From Darkness
to Hope

From Darkness to Hope

Prison Writings about Redemption

EDITED BY
Tuan "Mike" Doan

INTRODUCTION BY
Luis J. Rodriguez

LOS ANGELES, CA

Printed in the United States.

ISBN: 978-0-9838088-2-4

Book Design: Jane Brunette
Cover Art: Alfredo Mayorga

PUBLISHED BY:

Barking Rooster Books
PO Box 328
San Fernando, CA 91341

Contents

*A candle of hope is not intended
to overpower the darkness,
but to be a reminder
that darkness will not overpower me.*

Preface

A while back, I was a trainer/facilitator for four days of intense psychotherapy. Men came from around the country and parts of the world, such as England, Australia, and South Africa, to get a better understanding of themselves.

I remember three other facilitators and myself standing in the middle surrounded by close to thirty men. Most were intellectual, professional in their fields, such as doctors, lawyers, accountants, and military officers. A few were average working Joes. Their designer clothes were like neon lights telling the world their status in life. My heart was racing because this was my first time as a trainer. I felt so unprepared. Then a thin smile spread across my face. I knew what I needed to do.

I looked at my other facilitators and their faces were just as lost as mine. Our trepidations were palpable. I began to remove my shirt and asked other facilitators to do the same. When I dropped my shirt to the floor, I stood there in the designer tattoos that adorned my body, telling the world how tough I was. But deep inside I was just a shy insecure little boy that grew up poor and uneducated. I looked at the men surrounding me and asked them to take off their shirts and throw them on the floor. Slowly they all shed their designer clothes and revealed their bare skin.

"Underneath what you wear is flesh, bones, and hurts," I said, "We will try to dig deep into your emotional self, and help you heal old wounds and scars that were long ago hidden. We are all the same, each of us hurting in our own way."

In those four days of training, men cried tears of hurt. Others shouted out with voices of betrayal. Some cursed people that used them or took advantage of them. Those were four amazing days where people got to heal old wounds that have been repressed so well that they had long been forgotten. In the end, each man that came to us walked away with a better understanding of who they were. And that forgiving of oneself is the beginning of the healing process of forgiving others.

Everything starts with you.

The following stories and poems in these pages are a collection of experiences that emerged from broken homes, where men's dreams and hopes were either washed away by a constant rain of criticism or drowned in the ugliness of the streets. Dysfunctional households cause psychological traumas and impart warped views of love. These men had great potential but no one there to show them how to express themselves, and no available platforms to allow young minds the seeds of greatness to flourish. There was nothing to look forward to, but pain and destruction. They developed a survival mentality that benefited no one.

I hope that sharing these experiences may enlighten those who do not understand, but still seek to have an open mind. To those who feel there is no hope let them see that there is light at the end of the tunnel. I pray you take our short stories and poems and grow from these experiences so that you do not make the same mistakes we made.

I have already taken one life and caused so many broken hearts. But if I waste my life by doing nothing, then I have also taken my life.

ACKNOWLEDGMENTS: A special thanks to my wife and all the wives and families of countless inmates who remain long-suffering yet vitally important support systems. We pray these writings be of some consolation as you await the return of loved ones. Our deepest appreciation goes out to the sponsors and volunteers who, devoid of judgment, enter these facility grounds and benevolently extend helping hands to the classified reprobates of society. Also to the "inmates" who brought to life to this body of work, and those who inadvertently imparted to its production, we extend our immense gratitude. Striving to replace scrutinized yet false identities with hearts crafted from the wellness of positive change, your voices together are a glorious masterpiece ringing aloud from the canvas of these pages. All proceeds of this book's sales will go to nonprofit programs that help youth.

–*Tuan "Mike" Doan, California State Prison*
 Los Angeles County, Lancaster, CA

Introduction

For close to forty years, I've entered prisons and juvenile lockups to teach creative writing, do poetry readings, talks, and facilitate healing circles. I started in 1980 with my mentor, the late Manual "Manazar" Gamboa, in California's Chino Prison. Since then I've been to San Quentin, New Folsom, Soledad, and Lancaster state prisons, as well as county jails, juvenile halls and state juvenile facilities throughout California.

I've also done the same in Illinois, Michigan, Pennsylvania, Connecticut, Indiana, Ohio, Nebraska, North Carolina, Texas, New Mexico, Arizona, Nevada, Washington, Virginia, and Delaware. I've worked with organizations like Barrios Unidos, the William James Foundation, Insight-Out, Inside Out Writers, and the Alliance for California Traditional Arts. And because of my reputation in this field, I've entered high level prison institutions and juvenile facilities, or worked with adjudicated youth, in Mexico, El Salvador, Guatemala, Nicaragua, Argentina, Italy, and England. Why? For one thing, for what you have in your hands—words, thoughts, stories of trauma and trouble, but also redemption, prayers, restoration, and ultimately transformation.

I know people can change, even when the environment, be it poverty or prison, can stifle most healthy choices and capacities. This is the abundance Creator has given every human being—to generate and regenerate, and the resiliency to overcome all personal and social failures. Yes, many people don't make it. But why bother with God, spirit, and transcendence if this wasn't true for the vast majority of us under these and other circumstances?

Thanks to Tuan "Mike" Doan for helping make this book possible and to Barking Rooster Books for publication. I thank the California Department of Corrections and Rehabilitation, especially those at the California State Prison, Los Angeles County (Lancaster), for giving me this opportunity. And to the Alliance for California Traditional Arts for sponsoring my creative writing classes at Lancaster State Prison since 2016 as well as the Arts for Justice Fund for supporting the "Trauma to Transformation" project of Tia Chucha's Centro Cultural.

–Luis J. Rodriguez, author of "Always Running, La Vida Loca, Gang Days in L.A." and "It Calls You Back: An Odyssey Through Love, Addiction, Revolutions & Healing."

Bittersweet Memories

Many people I've met have been influential in shaping my personality. Many have given me the best moral values and advice while others a not-so-great self-destructive guidance that tends to get me in trouble. While I will never become who I want to be due to circumstances that have me serving life in prison, I do believe I'm a better person now than I will ever be.

My life has been a hard and dangerous road. I am serving 146 years to life and have been incarcerated for 18 years now. How I got here is probably due to my immaturity. I was rebellious back then. I didn't want to be like everyone else. I wanted to be different. I wanted to have an escape from an ordinary life. "The thing was to make your own rules, do your own thing, but make sure it's contrary to what society says or is" (Wideman 680). To me that meant joining a gang, which was my worst decision ever.

I grew up in South Central Los Angeles and had a big supportive and loving family. I really don't have a good excuse for why I joined a gang. All I can point to is my immaturity. My parents were hard working and always encouraged their children to pursue an education. What probably pushed me towards the gang life or hanging out with my friends was our poverty. I didn't have good clothes like the rest of the kids. I was embarrassed of the house we lived in. We had calendars up on the walls to cover up the holes in them. The furniture was arranged in a way that would hide the holes in the floorboards. If not, you could see the pipes and dirt underneath. From the outside you could see the yellow paint peeling off. The house was featureless. It was plain ugly.

The only good thing about our house was its location. It was right across the street from Bethune Park. There I would wait for all the kids to pass by when were released from Edison Jr. High, which was two streets down, so they wouldn't see where I lived. Later on I found out my brothers would do the same thing. Anyways, only my closest friends knew where I lived. We used to meet every day in this park to play sports or just joke around at the benches. For me this was a relief. It made life easier, less problematic. It was actually when we moved to our new home that I started having problems.

We moved to San Bernardino in 1991 when I was 15 years old. We moved there because my parents were buying a house. Houses in San Bernardino were cheaper than in L.A. While I was happy to be living in a decent looking home, I never knew that going to school would become a problem. You see, the biggest Hispanic gang in San Bernardino County was well established in my new high school, Pacific High. This gang made it a priority to get rid of any L.A. gang members that attended their high schools.

Hence, I would get into fights, mainly jumped until I got kicked out of the school district after two-and-a-half years of attending Pacific High School. Other guys from L.A. would get threatened or jumped and they wouldn't return. I felt I didn't have a choice. Education meant everything to me. I didn't want to end up like my dad, working his entire life for a low paying job. So I borrowed my sister's address in South Central and enrolled at Fremont High School. During this time, my dad still had his job at South Central. I would join him on the 80-mile drive to L.A. until I graduated.

The reason why I graduated from Fremont could be attributed to the good role models I had in my life. Besides my parents' encouragement, I have my sister Guadalupe to thank. She's the smartest one in the family—I always wanted to be as smart as her. Right now she's a schoolteacher with a Master's Degree. She is the reason why I took Algebra II, Trigonometry, Calculus, Chemistry, and Physics—just to prove I could do what she could.

Another person with a lasting impact in my life was my Edison Jr. High teacher, Mr. Lefferink. Besides history being my favorite subject, he told us something I've always kept in mind—the day has 24 hours and most people waste their free time doing nothing.

He said most people work eight hours or go to school and then do nothing else with the extra time to better themselves. He said people could use that extra time to learn new skills, or do something with it that will help them in the future. Thanks to him and my family, I never passed up any opportunities that came my way. This is why I graduated from college in prison.

The reason I did not graduate from college in the streets is because after I graduated from high school, I needed a break. I joined the U.S. Army Reserves. I came back after I was done with boot camp and AIT. I was ready for college, but messed up and got my girlfriend pregnant. The day I told her I wanted to break up with her because she was cheating on me, she told me she was pregnant. Hence, I got together with someone I hated and had to learn to love her again.

She moved in with us and I found a job. To me this was the right thing to do. I just couldn't imagine my kids growing up without a father. After I found a job where I worked 10 to 12 hours a day, five to six days a week, I decided to attend ITT Tech in my free time. I would go to ITT Tech for four hours a day, five days a week. I didn't enroll into a regular college because I didn't have the time for it. Anyhow, there was a brief interruption into my daily routine: I was arrested for an accessory after the fact on an "assault with a firearm on a person" charge. I got out the county jail in 1998, found me another job and picked up where I left off at ITT Tech. I figured, if I was going to be in debt, I might as well graduate. You see, I can be a good hardworking person and know what's right.

The problem is I hold grudges with everyone who wronged me. Like I said before, I was jumped throughout my school years at Pacific High School. But that's not all. I was also stabbed with screwdrivers in the street and pistol whipped. I was jumped on another occasion. I thought I was done. Their biggest error was letting me live. I wasn't so merciful.

I am now incarcerated for a murder and three murder attempts. Life in prison has been chaotic and problematic these past 18 years. It's hard to find rest and peace in a place like this. However, there have been a few bright spots that helped my development. For example, when I was in the county jail, I remember the first time I went to the hole. I ran into this white guy named Kaleb who became my friend. He's the one who got me into reading novels. Back there we had nothing to do all day so he let me borrow his books. He loaned me a John Grisham book and another one by Sidney Sheldon. From then on I fell in love with reading.

I've read hundreds of novels ever since, for "I came to enjoy the lonely good company of books" (Rodriguez 557). Years down the line, I was in the hole again, this time in Corcoran SHU. I was celled up with a guy I hated so much that I chose to ignore him most of the day. Let's just call this guy E.T. E.T. would like to argue and criticize me all day long, so I would grab my books and ignore him. It's also because of him that I started writing Spanish songs.

Writing songs gave me a distraction, tested my creativity, and gave me another reason to ignore this guy. However, ignoring E.T. would only make him madder until he finally asked me if I wanted to go at it with steel. I said, "Bring it." He didn't bring it. All he said was, "Oh, I see we are not getting along."

The next day E.T. put in a cell move—he moved a few cells down with one of my homeboys. He said it was better this way. I agreed. E.T. had beaten up his last cellmate. For some reason, he thought he would do the same with me. The only thing that stopped me from hurting this guy is our "prison rules," or the ones we have within ourselves. Other than that, I was just looking for an excuse to put hands on him. Now that I'm on the mainline or out of the SHU, I found out from two of his homies that E.T. is in protective custody. Like I knew all along, he was all bluff.

Life in prison has not been easy. Stabbings happen all the time. Then there are the racial riots that happen once in a while. Also disputes within one's racial group as well as correctional officers intent on making our lives miserable. Add to that the impotence of not being able to be there for your children when they need you. You can end up with a really stressed out individual.

However, I believe I came in with an advantage—I was better able to cope with this miasma we live in. Now, I am glad I lived in that house I grew up hating. Poverty toughened me up. In a way my enemies in the streets also did me a favor by all those beatings I took, which prepared me to the dangers I was to encounter throughout my sentence.

Most importantly, I believe I'm a better person now for I've come to understand all my errors and what I should have done instead. I have learned to be patient and think before I act. I am mellower now. I also understand I'm far from redemption. "I have a lot to hide. Places inside myself where truth hurts, where incriminating secrets are hidden, places I avoid, or deny most of the time" (Wideman 712). However, I believe I have made some progress— all the animosity I once had for my enemies is gone. One time, I even saved one of my enemies from the streets when he was getting stabbed up in the county jail.

As for my family, I am so grateful for the family God gave me. They have been real supportive. Not only have they looked after my needs, but those of my children as well. Being in a place where your life could be taken away from you any day has me aware: I cannot go away without letting my family know how I feel. I let them know how important they are to me and how much I love them in every letter. Finally, the education I have attained helped me realize a goal I thought beyond my reach. I always wanted to go to college. Now, I'm able to give tips to my kids who just started college, and share my essays with them. Nevertheless, none of this would be possible if it wasn't for these people in my life who gave me the motivation to keep my mind active, always wanting to learn more, and making something out of nothing.

Life in prison is not easy. Many gang members think they are just going to come in here and have a good time with their homies. If this was the case there wouldn't be so many SNY's (Sensitive Needs Yards) full of gang members who couldn't handle the pressure. Therefore, I'm grateful for all the people who gave me the strength and desire to persevere, for giving me something to live for, and most importantly, for helping me find myself.

I was sentenced to 146 years to life. I've been incarcerated since 1999. However, thanks to AB1308 I now have a board date of 2023. I just want to say to anyone—learn to value and appreciate everything you have. Some of us don't learn this until it's too late.

–*Casi Amezcua T-41989*

My Struggles Within

Sometimes I don't like looking at myself in the mirror. I be mad, upset, frustrated, and angry for being in this situation I'm in. I know I could've made something of myself, accomplished something. But here I am, sitting in prison, looking stupid mad at the world and everyone else for my decisions and mistakes. I have no one to blame but myself! My mom didn't encourage me, nor did my uncles, aunt, cousins, or friends. No white man made me.

Nobody but me.

I was a kid trying to be grown, trying to be like my uncles, cousins, and their friends. When in all actuality I should've stayed in school, got my education, played sports, listened to my mom and grandmothers! Now that I sit in this prison cell, with a life sentence, I wish I had listened.

All my family ever wanted was for me to grow up and become a responsible man who's educated with an honest legal job. To be someone who takes care of his family. Did I listen? No I didn't. Instead I chased fast money, I gang banged, sold drugs, broke into houses, stole, robbed—everything I didn't have any business doing, especially gang banging. I didn't realize that was the wrong path I was taking.

Well, honestly, I struggle with that because I knew it wasn't normal, but I did it anyway. Even though I was going to school (granny be tripping), I played high school football and basketball. My homies laughed at me because we hanged out late nights. I would leave saying I had to go to school in the morning. They made all kinds of jokes, even nicknamed me Professor. But I still went to school and gang banged, doing my thing. I thought I would do it all. Little did I know I was wrong.

Once I didn't pass my S.A.T. or A.C.T. when I turned 18. I knew I wasn't going to graduate on time because my ninth grade year I hardly ever went to school. School was keeping me from going to jail as a juvenile. I'm an adult now. I tried junior college, but my attention was elsewhere. By then I was full-time in the streets, living a life of crime. It was all fun, lots of women, money, shootouts, fights. I even had a part-time job.

Many people tried talking positive to me, but I didn't listen. I was trying to get more money, women, more drugs to sell, or a house to break into, somebody to rob, a rival gang to shoot at. Even though I was more into getting money, the gang banging held me back. That was my downfall.

No matter how much good you do, or how you think you could balance the two lifestyles, trust me—you can't. You're setting yourself up for failure. Gang banging is a job within itself, if you're really out there doing it. One mistake, just one, can cost you your life or freedom! I'm a prime example of how one bad decision can cost you everything.

After two years of running the streets, doing nothing with my life, I checked back into school, got a job, had my first child. Unfortunately, I was still hanging out, trying to stay relevant. Then all hell broke loose one night. Nine months later I'm in jail facing a life sentence, a year-and-a-half later I'm in prison with a 40-to-life sentence for a childish stupid mistake.

Now I'm mad upset at everybody. I'm starting fights with my enemies, my homies, whomever, disrespecting my girlfriends, arguing with my family. I just didn't care anymore. I always used to say I'd rather be dead than in prison with life. In my eyes a life sentence is death—you ain't never getting out.

When I ended up in prison, I got really mad, starting stuff for no reason. I didn't even want people looking at me for too long. If so, it became a problem. I can be real disrespectful when I want to be. I'm so far away from my family, a visit was out of the question. My girl came to see me but she didn't appreciate the things I said to her, so that became a problem. Misery loves company. Prison was making me miserable, bitter, angry!

I was in administrative segregation once, thinking about myself, my life, how it has turned out and about the decisions I've made and continued to make. I had just read this self-help book called "Tough Times Never Last But Tough People Do." I started reflecting about myself, soul searching, and realized I'm mad at everyone else for mistakes I've made. How lame is that? Nobody ever made me do anything—nor did they force me to. I did things, lived a certain lifestyle, out of my own ignorance.

I had every chance and opportunity to make something of myself. But I didn't take advantage. How can I blame someone else for me choosing to act crazy, childish, go around with this "I don't give a fuck" attitude? It was at that moment I realized the only person I should be upset with is the person I see when I look in the mirror. My decision making and thinking is the cause of this. Here it is: I'm sitting here behaving like someone I'm not because my own actions led me to be in prison.

Instead of being upset I should be trying to better myself. If I ever do get released, I'll should be mentally prepared and not make the same decisions I once did. First, I'd have to leave the gang mentality behind. Truthfully, this mentality is holding me back from becoming a mature man, worried about a street I don't even own. The streets don't love me! What you put into gang banging you don't get back in return.

At some point you have to understand where you went wrong. I hate I had to come to prison to understand I needed to leave that nonsense alone. There's a better way to live life without having to look over your shoulder everywhere you go, worried if the police are going to harass you, having to carry a gun everywhere. It's just too much of a headache; it's not normal or worth it! I know for a fact had I not been gang banging I wouldn't have come to jail. Going to school, getting a job... there is nothing wrong with that. I've done it and I know it. Who cares what everyone else thinks? You're responsible.

All the fast money and things will lead you to a fast death or a fast trip to prison. I sit back and regret a lot about the way I used to think, choices I've made. Being in prison you think about your life, every situation, a lot of things you did or were a part of, and you can see where you strayed off and took a wrong turn. If given a second chance you know what you would do differently. I know I would! First and foremost, I wouldn't be hanging out, gang banging, selling drugs, stealing, robbing, hanging with a negative crowd. I knew better than that in the first place. I was raised better than that. You need to surround yourself around positive people in a positive environment—this will bring out the positivity in you. Doing the right thing is not hard. Don't wait until you come to prison to wish you had just went to school, got a job, lived the simple life. Take advantage of the opportunity you have right now. There's no need to rush to be grown. Enjoy your childhood, live your life.

My uncle once said to me to be better than him. I now know what he meant after all these years. He didn't want me to experience prison. It's not a lifestyle or situation to be proud of, nor should you glorify it. Every day I wish I had just listened to my family that was telling me to stay in school, don't hang out with the wrong crowd, be your own man. Now I wish I would've listened. I wouldn't be here in prison having struggles within.

—*Kervin Bailey T-05246*

The Influence of Gang Culture on My Broken Adolescence

My name is Daniel Barry and I was born in Thailand. My biological father is from the United States and my mom wanted us to live in the US with him. But my father insisted we stay in Thailand. This was the cause for the separation of my mom and my biological father. As a result, she decided to go on her own. At the age of four, my mom brought me to the United States. She sought out a better life for us because she knew that the United States offered better economic and educational opportunities than living in Thailand.

When we came to the states, my mom met my step-dad. They were both immigrants from Southeast Asia so connecting on that level was the reason that brought them together. My step-dad came from Vietnam and he was a by-product of the Vietnam War. They eventually conceived two girls; I'm proud to be their big brother. We came to this country with nothing but the clothes on our backs.

Growing up, we were on welfare using W.I.C. and food stamps as a means to sustain ourselves with little or no income. There was a lot of stress placed on my mom and step-dad. Much of the stress stemmed from financial problems. My step-dad was a degenerate gambler, which didn't make the situation any better. This led my parents to become bitter with one another and caused them to be abusive toward us growing up.

When I say "us," I mean my two little sisters and I. But majority of the abuse was directed towards me because I was an easy target. Also because at times I didn't make the situation any better. I was a very active kid and wild at heart. I loved learning and sometimes would test boundaries because that's part of growing up.

My mind was active and full of curiosity; I got into a lot of trouble doing what kids do at that age. Growing up as a kid with constant verbal and physical abuse—being whipped with extension cords, bamboo sticks, slippers, open-handed smacks, or whatever my step-dad could get his hands on. I didn't realize this had a psychological effect on me. Eventually, the abuse took a toll and I was slowly changing.

I remember vaguely one day my mom and step-dad were arguing; it got really abusive. My step-dad put his hands on my mom and pushed her so hard that her hand smashed against the glass window shattering it. This cut the majority of her arm in the process. The ambulance was called and she was treated for her wounds.

I also remember another time my mom and step dad were in a heated argument because of me. He got so upset that he threw a bike at me, hitting my knee and cutting it. I still have that scar to this day.

Going through stuff like that, and seeing things being done to people I loved, made me develop a certain perspective on life. I grew up thinking that "might is right" and violence is acceptable. The only positive outcome of going through all that abuse was that I became very anti-spousal abuse. I hated seeing my mom go through the abuse. When I reached my teenage years, I finally got fed up with my step-dad's destructive behavior. I ended up getting into a physical altercation with him. From that day on, he stopped being abusive towards me. But I still hated him for what he did and could not tolerate being around him.

Growing up, and not having my biological father as a constant presence in my life, had its effect on me. My father is a merchant marine by trade; his work schedule takes him away for nearly nine months out of the year. That's hard on any family, especially when kids are involved.

My mother felt she was alone in this struggle. The lack of support had created resentment towards my dad. I remember one day when I was around the age of six or seven years old, my father came to visit. Being a kid, I was excited to see him just like any other kid would be when they haven't seen their parents for a long time. I was sad and upset when I knew he was getting ready to leave again, so I pleaded with him to stay. I wanted us to be together as a happy family, but he said he could not stay because of his work. It devastated me to the core. I felt heartbroken and threw a tantrum hoping that somehow he would stay. But nothing seemed to work.

From that moment on, I felt abandoned by my father. It took me years to finally process that situation. I came to realize that my father would rather choose his career over flesh and blood. This triggered multiple psychological issues for me such as anger problems—wanting to constantly get into physical altercations with other people and building a mental wall to keep individuals at a distance to avoid being hurt. I felt like I couldn't trust anyone fearing they would let me down, just like my father did. Since the time I was a young boy, l felt I wasn't good enough for my father, that he didn't love me enough to stay. You can imagine the point of view l was developing as a kid, how it could get carried into my adulthood. This way of thinking would later affect my decisions and the way I handled relationships in my life.

Home was supposed to make me feel safe and secure, but I didn't feel like that. I felt like an outsider in my own home. I was left alone at home a lot and I became accustomed to doing things on my own. I didn't have a father figure and there was really nobody to guide me or show me how to do things. This caused me to become stubborn and I developed a problem receiving advice from people.

I hated seeing my parents constantly arguing and hated the negativity they spewed at each other. l always had the impression that you shouldn't treat your loved ones by hurting them. This drove me to want to leave the house as often as I could. By this time, I was accustomed to being on the streets. I rather prefer this than being at home. I ran away from home many times. It started off for just a day, then slowly progressed into weeks. I would seek out friends so I could sleep over at their houses. I adjusted to sleeping on couches and floors.

As a juvenile delinquent, I ran into trouble with the law at the early age of twelve. My first criminal case was battery. By this time I became callous to violence due to my surroundings and the experience of abuse being done in my household. This made me believe it was okay to use violence to solve problems.

One day my best friend, whom I consider to be my brother, had joined a gang while I was incarcerated in a juvenile detention center (known as Eastlake, it's commonly called Central). When I called him, he told me what had happened to him. After I finished my phone call with him, I went back to my room and thought about what he had said. 1 became curious as to why my best friend would join the gang and who were this group of guys he was hanging with.

The first thing I did when I got released from juvenile hall was hang out with my best friend, who was my boy since first grade. At the age of thirteen, I eagerly joined the gang with him because I hated home. The older guys showed up and enticed me with a sense of belonging, easy money, accessibility to weapons, and the girls that came with this lifestyle. They glamorized this messed up world for me and I bought into it. When I made my decision to join, I was yearning to be accepted and wanted so badly to fit in that I didn't care about the consequences.

Soon I was heavily involved in the gang and the type of lifestyle associated with it. I used this as an escape to hide from the true pain I felt. It became easier to mask the truth. I became meaner and callous to the things I saw or dealt with on a day-to-day basis. In a sick perverted way, I felt more at home with these guys; I developed a warped sense of loyalty to them. At the time, I felt accepted by these guys and I would have gladly laid down my life for them.

I didn't care if I died, or the next person for that matter. There was total disregard for human life. I felt like people didn't care about me, so why should I care about them? I know this sounds absurd and stupid, but back then I didn't care. I was psychologically damaged. I wanted to fit in so bad it felt good to be accepted.

I just happened to choose the wrong path, which was negative and caused so much anguish.

While living this lifestyle, I dealt drugs because I got older and needed to support myself. I wanted to have nice things and not rely on asking my mom or anyone else for money. I started off hustling small amounts of drugs, mostly cannabis, and from time to time crystal meth. From selling dime sacks to dub sacks, I moved on to selling half ounces and whole ounces, then pounds of cannabis.

I sold Methamphetamine in eight balls mostly. I didn't really want to sell this because it was too much of a hassle dealing with "tweakers." It was a dangerous occupation. I heard stories of people getting robbed for their merchandise or being set up. I started carrying a firearm everywhere I went for protection. I was carrying firearms regardless because I was a gang member, but the real reason was for selling drugs.

I carried firearms like 9 mm's, 38's, or .22 mm's, depending on the situation at hand. I had all types of guns at different times. At one point I even had a MAC 11 with an extended clip. I was making good money at the time for a teenager. Because I was accumulating all this money, I was becoming obsessed with this lifestyle. I saw all these people struggling to make ends meet—working two jobs at times and going to school to get ahead in life. I thought to myself that this is way easier than what those people were doing. I could do this for the rest of my life. Forget school and forget college! This was just another reason I used to justify what I was doing. I rationalized what I was doing, which sounded logical in my mind.

I received large amounts of income from selling drugs. However, I didn't want to raise suspicions from my mom, who would start asking annoying questions. I got a job working at my uncle's pet shop. My boss was flexible and I enjoyed working there because I love taking care of animals.

On November 26, 2005, I made a horrible decision. I gave no second thoughts about the consequences or the impact it would make on all the people around me. My mentality was "get them first before they get me." On that night, I committed the act of first-degree murder and attempted murder on two human beings with total disregard. I was callous and indifferent; I stayed like that for a long time.

Once I got convicted and sentenced for my crimes, I was sent to prison to serve the rest of my life there, confined to a concrete box with limited things to do and having other people telling me what to do, when to shower, when to eat, where to sleep, and when to go outside. It's horrible! All the simple things in life I took for granted, I could no longer do again—like take a long shower, open the refrigerator when I feel like it, walk barefoot in the sand and feel the sand between my toes. Or walk on carpet, go to the movies, eat at a restaurant, or even drive a car. All these things were gone and in its place was concrete and coldness. I developed a mental shield to cope with my wants and desires; I adapted to my new environment, to deal with it the best way I could.

I was still ill mannered toward other inmates and correctional officers, constantly getting into fights because I wanted to prove myself. I also lacked the social skills to express myself. This caused me to be aggressive to those around me.

As the years went by, I grew older and wiser in prison. I met real good individuals who traversed the same path I took and learned things the hard way. They pointed out my flaws and where I was heading. At first, I didn't want to listen to their constructive criticism because I was stubborn. I refused to accept the reality of things.

Eventually what they were trying to tell me sunk in. I experienced a different outlook on life. I began to immerse myself in positive things, to expand my horizons. I noticed all the bullshit I allowed myself to get into and compromise what I really was. I thought back to the first two years of my incarceration and many of the people who I associated with. I put in much work with them. I actually put my life on the line for some of these people. But they didn't care. At the time, it pained me when I came to this realization.

This gang culture is a very cold world with no blanket; it's cut-throat with little remorse. Some people can handle this extreme lifestyle while others can't. I hate to say it, but it's nothing but a rat race for crumbs. At the same time, I have met some really solid individuals. I would try my best to have them step away from the negativity. I wouldn't want them to die or go down for someone else's stupidity. When I came to this realization, I slowly did things to step away and transformed my mentality. This is something you don't just do right away, like it's an on-off switch—especially when you have become accustomed to having a certain point of view for so long. It's hard to break that lens and reconstruct it into something else better.

In January of 2011, I put myself in a position where I ended up in Administrative Segregation Unit (also known as Ad Seg for short). Ad Seg is a place where they housed those who have violated the rules or those who committed extreme acts of violence on others. It's basically a concrete box where they strip away majority of your personal properties and human contact. While back there, we were allowed to have reading materials like books and magazines. I decided to turn this concrete box into a place of learning and growing instead of a place of anguish and hell.

I utilized my time and started to draw in there. I drew models from pages of magazines that used them to advertise perfumes or make-up products. I immersed myself deeply into drawing because I found that this could be meditative for me. I loved it. I had no formal training, just too much time on my hands and determination.

Drawing opened the door for me to see this newly discovered ability as an essential skill that no one can take away. I analyzed how I could use this new ability, and the opportunities available, to support my family and myself so I wouldn't have to resort to criminal behavior. I envisioned becoming a tattoo artist as a result of looking through countless tattoo magazines. I became determined to make this my profession. I saw this as a way out of the hood and the bullshit I associated myself with.

I practiced drawing almost every day while in Ad Seg. When

I was finally released from there, I started making greeting cards for money. I made birthday cards, mother's day cards, father's day cards, and cards for any major holiday and occasion.

Eventually, I acquired paints and taught myself how to paint. All the artwork I did that I didn't sell, I sent home to make a portfolio for me to see my progress as an artist. Plus, I saw this as a resume for myself when I applied for jobs that are art-related.

With society becoming increasingly accepting of tattoos, getting employed, and staying employed, as a tattoo artist would be no problem. Besides from tattooing, I could paint and sell my art as an extra source of income. With this realization, I now can't imagine myself doing anything else in my life. I don't have to resort to criminal activities for income. I can create beautiful art instead of destroying beautiful things; I can make people happy instead of sad.

I also disciplined myself into reading books. That was one of the best things I could have done in prison. I realized how much I love books and the many hidden knowledge written in books, which people don't give enough credit to. Reading books are part of my gateway into the realm of possibilities. The more I learned, the better I can handle situations and solve problems. It's ironic how I was one of those people who hated reading books. I didn't want to pick one up because I had this logical reasoning "Why pick up a book when I can just watch it?" I am extremely happy and fortunate to understand the importance of books, for this newfound hope and outlook on life. I have been able to do things outside of my comfort zone. I've been able to be myself without feeling my peers are judging me.

Now that I have come to this epiphany, and accepted that my old ways of living wasn't promising or no longer suitable, I signed up for self-help classes so I can fix my character defects. I implemented some of the lessons I learned from the self-help groups. This process helped me see things in a different perspective. Looking back on all of this, I came to realize how dangerous my life had been—it's crazy to think a teenager or any other adolescent should have this lifestyle.

For those who are reading this right now, I hope what I shared here is being taken to heart, that it may change your life in a positive and meaningful way.

–*Daniel Barry F-66143*

Taking Away the Innocent

Options strangled by the environment, influences that disregard and regard innocence as weakness, or susceptibility to fall victim to what one is surrounded by, should be eradicated. Some are stripped of this wide-eyed view, which we all are granted, by varying means early as children. Would you consider abuse traumatizing to a child's perception, though it be done under the intention of giving the kid an advantage in life by being aware of the world they are about to enter?

When is young too young to be made aware of what is going on around them so they have time to adjust? This is the justification in parenting under harsh and strenuous conditions. Every era has had trying circumstances, where the adults have the difficult task of protecting their child and at the same time preparing them for what they will walk into as they leave the safe confines of home.

As time changes, the world gets bigger and less hospitable for the doe-eyed "gullible" young. We teach our young to beware strangers for they might take you away. This is a hazard in most communities, yet in the urban municipal there are more predators and pitfalls than just the occasional rapist or child molester. We have guns, gangs, rampant disease, and drugs to contend with on a daily basis. So as a parent do you know these are the conditions your children will be raised in, play in, be taught in? When do you decide they need to be made conscious of the truth about what they may encounter so that they will not fall prey? There are no right or wrong answers; it is subjective. We regard our children's maturity, however young they may be. Yet our ability to perceive can't be predicted. We all progress and grow mentally at different speeds. It's a guessing game in supplying a child with a draught of reality that shall alter their whole way of viewing everything. We can only hope it is the correct thing to do.

At six years old, my best friend's twelve-year-old sister took my innocence; she stripped nude, opened her legs, and invited me inside her. At eight years old, my innocence taken by a friend of the family, who had been trusted to babysit my then five-year-old brother and me. He invited me into the bathroom and put a marijuana pipe to my lips and told me to inhale—my brother's uncle made bets on whether I would cough or not.

At ten years old, my innocence taken, listening through a cracked door as my mother and stepfather argued—the words unclear, the tone aggressive. I watched my mother attack him, and then watched her propelled into the air. I had my home and family taken away by my stepfather's indiscretions and my mother's inability to accept them. At eleven years old, my innocence taken by my uncle, ducking, crawling, and peeking around the edges of our couch and the corner of the center divide in our studio apartment. My mother held me close as I watched him. Old English malt liquor seeped through her pores as she told me her way of providing for me, other than the county check, was selling crack cocaine. She had sold some to my uncle. She told me I may see this as wrong, but reality was he would have went out and bought it elsewhere. Why shouldn't we keep that financial gain in-house?

At twelve years old, my innocence taken by my incessant need of my peers' approval. I was arrested for stealing a bike out the back of a truck that had pulled over in the front of my building. I was unaware it was a police operation, meant to lure someone's attention, enticing them into stealing the truck.

At thirteen years old, my innocence taken by my drunken father as he stabbed me in the lip with a Bic pen. I stood up to him as he proceeded to beat me, striking me in the nose with the palm of his hand, striking me with the palm of his hand in my mouth, tackling me to the ground and attempting to break my leg. Disowned by his parents for not apologizing to him because he got arrested. In my grandmother's opinion, I had a smart mouth and probably deserved the treatment I received. Running away to what I thought was the safe arms of my mother, to an environment where to eat we sold crack cocaine to addicts and committed home invasions. Forced into the role of a man as my mother's boyfriend took her head and struck it against the steering wheel of their 69' Impala. He bit her and punched her face for she had embarrassed him by beating up a woman he cheated on her with. Forced to choose between taking my mother's place or equalizing the circumstances and equipping myself with a firearm.

I chose the pistol.

Fourteen years old, my innocence taken—was it with the five girls I engaged in random sex with, getting one pregnant only to have her abort it before I was aware she was contracting gonorrhea from someone else; was it waking to my mother having sex beneath my bed, on the floor, as her boyfriend's younger homie watched while he ate my cereal. Or was it my need to sell crack cocaine on a daily basis.

It could have been having random pistols aimed in my face, shot in my direction, being robbed at gunpoint, having to fight grown men for being a Crip gang member in a Blood neighborhood. Maybe it was the brains from the store clerk splattered on the bags I witnessed in a robbery. Fifteen years old, my innocence taken as I pull the trigger of a .22 caliber revolver, the bullet striking the face of an innocent man and watching as the blood shoots from every orifice in his head.

I really can't say when my innocence was actually stripped away from me—or if I was ever granted the opportunity to see through those childish eyes, jaded by the chaos that surrounds our lives. My environment, the era I was born and raised inside of, the influences and mis-education I received from life and from those there to guide me. This all served to alter my perception—whether to shield me from the worst or inadvertently subjecting me to the trauma before I was equipped to deal with what that brought.

—Ira Durante Benjamin T-74257 (Excerpt from: "Bred to Chaos, Child of the 80's, A Lost Generation: 80's Babies"

When Intentions are Well Wishes

I chose my path—as treacherous as it has been. Pitted and stuck with life-altering ruts, which diverted me from optimizing the limited opportunities I was offered that others around me did not have. Squandered, because I couldn't recognize them for what they were at the time. I mistook my family wanting to foster me to distant relatives in the Midwest as them trying to pawn me onto some people that were strangers to me. They were taking me away from all that was familiar, separating me from my mother, who I thought I was meant to protect. If I weren't there to do so, what would happen to her?

This is how I saw it—they didn't care about my feelings, my misgivings, like I was a nuisance they needed to get rid of. This enforced the isolation I felt, with nobody to relate to but those engaged in the same felonious street activities causing this discourse. My vision obscured by personal perspective. I was unable to see they didn't know what to do. They felt me slipping away and didn't know how to reach me. They felt they were helping, presenting me with stability as they ambushed me and made plans to ship me to my previous absent father. A man whom I despised for not being there for me when I needed him, for not teaching me the workings of a man, for allowing me to look up to another man, who I called Dad, only to have him tell me I wasn't good enough to occupy his time when he no longer was tied to my mother—even though he was in the role as father for ten years.

I blamed my father for my mother degrading herself because I knew she loved him. I somehow knew what she was searching for, without liking it, that it was my father. Everything I hated about myself I attributed to him. For he was the one who abandoned me. His responsibility. His first-born son. He left me to a teenage mother that didn't know how to raise me into a man. I couldn't see he was a child too when he helped make me. I couldn't understand things from another's perspective. I just knew what I felt, how things affected me.

As I rode in that car with this stranger, his girlfriend, my half-baby-brother in his car seat, tears ran down my face. My eyes stared at the cars we passed on the freeway on our way to what was supposed to be my stability. In my heart I'm this wolf and I'm howling, discontent, chafing at the disconnection from my environment. How did my family think this was going to work? How! I had gotten used to fending for myself, making my own rules, doing what I wanted when I wanted—in essence what I thought being a man was about.

Therefore when this stranger, who had been absent for the most part of the thirteen years I had been on this earth, attempted to implement rules, structure, responsibilities, family values, discipline, it was ludicrous to me. Hypocritical really. I thought—how could this man teach me these aspects when he had never exhibited an ounce of those things toward me? In a tyrannical way he tried to bend me to his will—a wolf taken out of the wild into a domesticated setting.

I pulled away and fought any form of domestication and cohesiveness presented to me. When we ate together at the table, as a family, I'd say, "I'm not hungry, don't like your food, no thank you, you are not my family." When we read Bible verses together, go to church together, I'd say, "I'm not religious, I don't believe in the same things you do." When he tried to get me a hair cut, look presentable, "fuck that—my hair is long, my pants hang off my ass because I'm not you, and I don't care what the world thinks."

Whatever my father said to do I'd do the opposite. I wanted nothing to do with him. I hated when we shared a moment of happiness together. It gave me a glimpse of what we could've had. But now I seen it as too late, that it would be temporary, that I would be pushed away again if I opened myself to believe this was my home.

My father was an abusive, alcoholic, steroid-fueled bodybuilder—he had a predisposed hair trigger temper without the 'roids. I watched him once, in a temperamental state, beat his handicapped girlfriend, mother to his second born son, as she called out to me for help. I ignored her, not wanting to be involved. Not wanting to accept this was my life. This was what people perceived as stability? I ignored what was happening—it wasn't me. It wasn't my concern. How ironic how things work.

Another time my father beat me because, in a drunken state, he called the house pretending to be a man calling for a date with his girlfriend. He then told me his true identity and asked why would I not tell a man calling for his girl that she had a man!

"Well, that's not my business. It doesn't have anything to do with me."

Needless to say, he took exception to that and came home and proceeded to beat me. He bloodied my face, scarred me forever, inside and out, as my neighbor looked on in horror. His girlfriend, awakened by the disturbance, gave me the opportunity to slip away. I called my mother's mom, who then called the police. They arrested my father as he tried to flee.

His girlfriend, however, told the police whatever I told them was a lie. She said I—all of 5'6" and 130 pounds—attacked my 6'1" and 250-pound father. He stayed in jail for a week. She picked him up when I didn't press charges. He came home and told me he would never touch me again. I ran away three days later.

I've wondered at times what it is we are supposed to learn from the tragedies we experience. Is it just supposed to make us stronger? Give more scars to carry into our future? Make us feel alone amongst those we are supposed to be closest? Feel threatened in what should be safety? Realize we can't trust, that we are less than what deserves respect, common courtesy, human compassion, and consideration?

Or is it to give us a perspective so in the future we are able to protect ourselves against those experiences repeating, but also that we can understand and relate to those around us? To see ourselves in each other's faces, filled with the same blank stares or smiles we wear as masks? So we can no longer disconnect and say it's not me or I don't care.

—Ira Durante Benjamin T-74257

Mother of Mine

Hello, lovely mother of mine. Well, I'm writing you this letter to let you know I forgive you. The reason why I'm expressing this is because I'm in this class called Houses of Healing, a real good group. We had to write a letter to someone you can truly forgive and you came into mind. Mom, even though when I was a kid and you were in the bathroom getting high and I felt like I was alone being neglected, I forgive you. Mom, even though when I was a young child and I wanted you to acknowledge me and you didn't, I forgive you. Mom, even though I didn't have any parental guidance and I was able to do whatever I wanted, I forgive you. Mom, I recently talked to you about all this time I got and you felt like you had to take blame because you asked me to take a deal. Mom, I forgive you. You are not to blame for the choices I made. I put myself in here and no matter how our past was, I'm proud of you today. As I said before, I forgive you.

Truly,
Your Son Ernie

—*Ernie Boon T-50834*

From Darkness to Hope

At three years old, my mother caught my dad cheating. She came home crying, waking my twin sister, my one-year-old brother, and me. She then brought us into the kitchen, turned up all the gas on the stove and oven, took out a birthday candle, and placed it into a coffee cup. She put my sister and I in front of the oven while she held my little brother on her lap. The fire department found us all passed out, miraculously—the candle she lit had gone out.

At five years old, a few days before Christmas, mother tried to put up a small plastic Christmas tree. My dad came out the room and tore it down; he said we don't celebrate Christmas in this house and there's no Santa Claus.

At seven, I witnessed my mother and father shoot up heroin in their arms. I saw my mother and father O.D. off heroin and almost die. My twin sister and I were born addicted to heroin.

At eight, I saw my mother being raped. I was too scared to do anything about it. I went back to my bed and played sleep until my mother came and got us out of the room. The man broke her nose, blackened both her eyes, and knocked out two of her teeth. My father was in prison at the time for drugs. I was doing bad in school—kids picked on me because I couldn't read.

At nine, I got into fights, whipped often, suspended from school. I used to beat myself up when I didn't get my way. My mother was doing heroin real bad by then. She sold herself for drugs. At times she would leave us at home and be gone for days. My sister and I would go looking for her. We wouldn't tell anyone we were alone. We took care of our then five-year-old brother and two-year-old sister. Then my mother would pop up, like nothing ever happened.

At 10, my daddy got out of prison and everything seemed fine at first. Then he started doing heroin again; he got sent back to prison for five years for robbery. My first arrest was for breaking into a school. I used to break into peoples' home just to eat; I'd steal food so I could feed my siblings. We were on county aide, but all the money my mother got went into her arms.

At 11, I stole car batteries and sold them to buy food and to help my mother buy heroin so she wouldn't be hitting us. When she didn't get her fix, she would take it out on us. She blackened my eye many times. She would say hurtful things like, "You stupid just like your daddy" and "I should have sat up when your head came out."

I would have done anything to make her happy and love me.

At 12, my daddy got out of prison again. He then sold drugs, including weed. He was getting drunk; he and my mom fought all the time. My mom was still doing heroin and my daddy stopped, but he started smoking P.C.P. Then I told him mother was a prostitute when he was in prison. He looked at me and knocked me out. Told me he knew and for me to stop being a tattletale, to never say anything about what I saw or what I heard.

At 13, my daddy was trying to play daddy and I wasn't listening. He got mad and hit me, knocking me out. He knocked me out so many times I lost count. By then I was looking at girls and trying to talk to them, but I didn't know what to say. Girls would laugh at me, and give me the wrong phone number. I graduated from elementary school but didn't know how to read, write, or spell. I entered junior high school with no education.

The gang picked on me. I would walk to my classroom and they picked on me because I had on old clothes. I'd walk out the classroom. When the gang started picking on me I began taking a knife to school for protection. When a gang member came by me, I would take my knife out and let him know I would hurt any one of them if they kept messing with me. They laughed and said they were going to kill me first. I'd say to them, "we will kill each other." I got jumped on a lot of occasions. I became scared to go back to school. So I hit a teacher at the school just to get kicked out. My daddy beat me with a golf stick; he broke my hand for hitting the teacher and getting kicked out of school.

At 14, I started smoking marijuana. I drank and joined the rival gang of the gang that jumped me. Now my homies and I were beating them up.

At 15, I got my house shot up. I went right back and shot up some of their houses. I got shot in the leg. My daddy had enough of me and started hitting me. I was so scared, but I tried to defend myself and hit him back. As soon as I hit him I knew I shouldn't have done that. I started running away from him. He chased me down and hit me in the back of my head and knocked me out; I fell on top of the broken dishes. I came to feeling a foot stomping the back of my head. He left a deep scar running across my cheek. I ran to my mother's room and got her gun. I shot twice and hit my father in the right shoulder and the wall. I did it because of all the abuse he inflicted on me and my siblings, but mostly me and my twin sister. He used to knock her out too. One time he hit her in the head with a skillet and put a gash on her head. We would lie to the doctors about our injuries when we went to the hospital. I wanted to hurt him like he hurt my siblings and me.

At 16, I started living with my grandmother, my daddy's mother. I was going to school and playing football. I was good at football. My grandmother encouraged me; she made me promise to stay in school and she'd come and watch me play. I was doing really well in school. Everything was going good for me. Then my grandmother died of a heart attack and everything went out of control. I dropped out of school and started hanging out with my homies again. I lived on my own, sold drugs, robbed people, stole things. I did what I wanted to do. I got arrested a few times and sent to probation youth camps. Nobody knew what I was going through, and I didn't know how to tell anyone. I was angry, deceitful, impulsive, aggressive, out of control, and a destructive kid.

I know I cannot wash away all my wrongs. But I have worked hard to re-define who I truly am as a person. I want to be remembered as someone who truly cared about others and loved helping others in need.

—*Kenneth Denson D-02243*

The Final Goodbye

It was close to midnight when I entered the long hall of Orange County Juvenile Hall. The lime floor shined, smelling like pine, so clean. The tier quiet. I approached the counselor who sat behind a high desk counter and gave him my name. He handed me a plastic bag and told me to strip down to my underwear and throw my belongings and clothing inside the bag. Once I did that, he gave me a roll of clean clothes, which consisted of briefs, socks, a dark blue T-shirt, and pants. He pointed in the direction of a row of showers and said, "Five minutes!"

The hot water felt good. It had been days since I'd showered. I stayed there long after I was done. The pounding on the glass window got my attention. Once dried and dressed, I gingerly walked towards one of the two phones. I picked up the phone and began dialing my house number, but stopped dialing after punching the first four digits. It was already late and everyone would be asleep, I reminded myself. I hung up the phone and returned to the counselor who handed me a plastic comb. I guess he thought I needed it! "You're in room two. That way!" he pointed with his chin. He pushed a button on a board behind him. Clank! The lock released, the door opened a few inches. I thought for sure that had woken everyone, but no prying eyes were on the long Plexiglas windows as I casually combed my hair and strolled coolly to my assigned room.

It's easy to be cool when you've been here before and know the "get down." Yeah, I thought I was cool. I did six days the last time for joyriding. Cool people don't walk, their feet glide.

The nightlight was already on, which I had no control of. I pulled the door closed, to my long time-out. I didn't slam the door hard enough and it sprang open. "Harder!" the irate voice of the counselor rolled the hall. That took my coolness back a notch. I put some back arm into my second attempt and the door slammed shut with a clink. I checked out my small concrete tomb. The walls were filthy with foul smearing spit and other body fluids. The smells were rancid. Every breath I took was a challenge not to gag. I made my bed and lay down. I was extremely tired but sleep wouldn't come. So many thoughts were racing through my mind; it was like a dam bursting, refusing to let my tired body rest.

I thought about my mother and how I had let her down again. The more images I saw of her sad disappointed face in my head, the more it stressed me out. I tried to avoid thoughts of my mom by thinking of the good time I just had with my friends. A moment ago, my homeboys and I were hanging out at my homegirl's birthday party. She no doubt was worried and wondering when we will bring back her parent's car.

I thought about my two homeboys, Hieu and Tu, who were in the same car with me. Lucky bastards, I told myself. They are probably walking back to the party now, or maybe already there. "If you weren't driving, you wouldn't be arrested!" one of the arresting officers told me. A thin smile spread across my face as I thought of my two road-dogs. I should've pointed it out to the officers at the time that both of my homeboys could've played roles of "Oompa Loompas" on Charlie and the Chocolate Factory. Hieu was eleven and Tu was twelve and both could pass as third graders. I was bigger than most of my homeboys—at fourteen my legs could reach the pedals and my eyes were above the steering wheel. I was the least likely to get pulled over, so we all believed.

My thoughts now floated toward my girlfriend, Mai, and my heart began beating faster. She was gorgeous, stunning, and I was shocked when she asked me out. "Me? Are you sure?" I wanted to ask her. We hardly talked. How about all those guys in school who bunched around her, showering her with compliments and unyielding attention? My homeboys and I were too cool to flock around her like those schoolboys.

We'd do it after school and the opportunities were few. My face felt hot, flushed with embarrassment as I recalled our first date. We agreed to meet inside the skating rink. Without money

I had to sneak in while she bought a ticket. Such a good girl!

After three days of being locked up in solitary confinement, which is the duration of the orientation process, I was finally moved to regular unit and allowed out for one hour of dayroom. After the hour was up, I dragged my feet back into the abyss of loneliness and boredom.

When I went before the judge, he gave me a quick glance and with a no-nonsense tone, sentenced me to four months for joyriding with a promise I would go to Y.A. (Youth Authority) the next time I saw him. The ignorance of youth, and the bad choices I continued to repeatedly make, led me to the same judge. This next time I was sentenced to six years in Y.A. By the time I got out my eight-year-old youngest brother had turned eleven and my other brother turned fourteen. My mother was now forty-six; time lost and memories never created.

Two months later, I was in a car with one of my friends. As he drove to pick up his girlfriend from work, we were pulled over. I was taken in for being in contact with a "gang member." I didn't sweat it because I knew he wasn't a gang member. Besides I hadn't even committed a crime, so the most I expected to get was three to six months. My assumptions were wrong. I was hit with eighteen months. I still told myself it was no big deal. With "good time" I would be out in a year. I was wrong, again. By the time I was paroled, three years had passed. I was paroled on a Friday, but because I was a "high-risk parolee," my parole officer wouldn't release me until after the weekend.

"They killed Irvine!" my schizophrenic eldest brother excitedly shouted at me as I walked through the back door.

"What the hell are you talking about?" I stated irately. I continued walking not caring for his answer, and not in a mood to have a discussion with his mind.

"They killed Irvine Friday night. Shot him four times. You better be careful!" he called out his warning towards my fading back.

I went into my room and closed the door, shutting out any more warnings. I was paroled but I did not feel free. There were many thoughts in my head. I already knew that three of my home-boys had been killed months ago; two had been badly shot. I took in a deep breath, expecting the air of freedom to taste better. It didn't.

The phone rang. Before I picked it up I knew it was for me. Word travels fast and I knew they'd be calling.

"Hello! Yeah, it's me."

"Irvine's dead!" one of my homeboys told me. My mind went numb, my crazy brother was right. My mind didn't register a majority of the things my homie was saying but I managed to catch the last part. "He was shot four times."

I didn't care if he was still on the line when I hung up—I needed to lie down. This is surreal. Only a couple of months ago, I had spoken to Irvine on the phone. We reminisced about the good simple days when we didn't have nice cars, fancy clothes, and we didn't go around talking smack. All we wanted to do was ditch school and hang out with each other. "It's crazy Batman," Irvine said. His voice sounded tired and weary. "Now all the new young homies drive around in their expensive cars, that their parents bought, and act tough!"

"Just step back and let them learn life's lessons the hard way!" I had said, hoping Irvine would stop putting himself in front of a bullet for them.

We talked about other things and Irvine mentioned his desire to attend college and change his lifestyle to ensure he'd be there for his four-year-old gorgeous baby girl, whom he adored.

I lay there recalling other memories. I could clearly see Irvine's face as if it were yesterday. How he stormed up to me during our middle school recess. His face flashed with anger as he shouted to me that someone had pushed him. I looked into his thirteen-year-old face full of anger and excitement with tears streaking down his gentle but sharp eyes, and told him, "Don't trip! Show me who it was!" I wrapped my left arm around his hundred pound narrow frame and marched toward the bully.

My phone rang again, taking me out of my reverie. Another homeboy calling to give me more details. I wanted to slam the phone down and tell him to go hang himself with his details.

"Yeah, we couldn't help him. He was bleeding too much and the cops were coming!"

So, my road-dog laid dying, giving his blood for those he loved, but not one stayed to comfort him. He died alone. I hung up on him too.

I picked the phone back up to call my little homeboy, Little Tinh. L.T. was more than a homeboy—he was more like a little brother to me. He has this enchanting way of making people move to his beat. He has the cool handsome look of Johnny Depp without the mustache. He's extremely intelligent, articulate, and could converse about any subject. He has this nerdy confidence in his speech that makes you want to listen. When you got mad at L.T., he would flash his easy smile and let out a soft laugh that sounded more like a giggle. The innocent smile along with his boyish giggle made apologies less wanting. It worked on me many times. That's why we bonded so easily. I needed him for tomorrow.

I drove to his house the next day. His little sister let me in. At first I didn't recognize him lying curled in the middle of the living room floor. His pajamas hid his bony body. His face was gaunt with dark shadows underneath both eyes. He looked like a starving vampire. He opened his mouth to tell me that he was tired and needed a few more hours of sleep.

"We don't have time!" I told him, resisting my temptation to shout.

"Just an hour," he pleaded. "I haven't slept in four days!"

"I don't care. Get up!" I half dragged him to his feet and he lazily went and got dressed.

Little T sunk into my car seat like the dead welcoming the coffin. He stared out the side window with both his hands tucked between his legs. He was trying to avoid eye contact with me knowing how much I disliked homies doing drugs. Drugs had taken a toll on him and it saddens me to see him like this. The inside of the car was already warm but I turned the heater up more for him. He felt more comfortable and began speaking softly, staring ahead. "Man, that dude that killed Irvine, I was in Juvenile Hall with him and I kicked his ass. He can't fight!" I could see through the side of my eyes that he had turned to look at me maybe hoping I would give him a compliment. I didn't.

I put in my favorite tape. Bon Jovi was rocking my heart with "Blazing Glory." I turned it up and started to sing along softly, thinking of Irvine.

"I woke up in the morning and I raised my weary head. I got an old coat for a pillow and the earth was last night's bed. I don't know where I'm going only I know where I've been. I'm a devil on a run, a six gun lover, a candle on the wind." The guitar rocked and I listened as I drove.

It was a warm Tuesday afternoon. The sun was high and bright. I stood there dressed in my black pants and long dark blue dress shirt. The shaking started from my legs and slowly took over my entire body. I wasn't cold but I couldn't stop trembling. It happens sometimes when I am nervous or mad, but at the moment I felt neither. Little T was standing next to me. I turned to look at Little T and was glad he was here. There weren't many road-dogs of mine left and he was one of the special few I truly cared for and loved. His clothes hung loosely over his body. I hoped L.T. hadn't noticed my trembling. If he did, he didn't let it be known. His gloomy sad eyes stared at the group of Irvine's family and acquaintances. The coffin was lowered and their sniffling and crying could be heard from where I stood, thirty feet away.

I watched as Hieu began to walk over to L.T. and me. His steps were heavy. Gone was the usual confident bounce in his small frame. I smiled as an image broke loose from my subconscious. It was a very long time ago and we were only kids then. I remembered Hieu standing atop a tree stump so he could reach the older girl that had finally agreed to let him give her a peck on the cheek, after pestering her all day.

Hieu was brave that day. We all wanted her to reject his request so we could crush his heart. Cruel friends we were when opportunity called for it, not caring about the insecurity or therapy needed to overcome such rejection.

It looked strange seeing him walking towards me without his cousin Tu. Those two were inseparable, even in Y.A. they were in the same building.

Hieu came up to me and we shook hands with an arm hug. My trembling stopped. He gave L.T. a cool handshake. The look in Hieu's eyes spoke clearly his silent thought, "How had it all gone so wrong? So many dead and so many locked up." I wanted to tell him that we were still boys trying to be men not sure what to do, confused in the game of "Cowboys and Indians" with real bullets. I wish I had the answer, or someone wiser to answer all my questions.

I broke into the conversation by asking him about his cousin. "He's fighting a heavy one. The D.A. wants to give him life."

"That's heavy," I sighed, but wondered what's heavier than losing your life, literally.

We chatted a little longer before he walked away. I wanted to call Hieu back and tell him that everything would be all right!

While Hieu and I spoke, Irvine's family and acquaintances slowly slipped away to their cars. L.T., the rest of the homeboys and homegirls, and I moved in to take their place. I stood there with my thoughts, staring at the mound of flowers on top of Irvine's freshly covered resting place. One of my homeboys brought out a large white wreath he had designed, or requested to be made, with our neighborhood's name in the middle and placed it on top. Looking at the wreath made me irritated, "Who are we?" "Are we better than the mother who lost a son or a sister without her brother?" The neighborhood took him from them.

My trembling picked up again and I was tempted to grab that wreath and fling it away. I blamed the wreath for my irritation but deep down inside I blamed myself. I wasn't there when Irvine needed me; I failed him. Damn my trembling for making me look weak! "Why can't you stop?" I scanned my homeboys' faces. The more I looked, the more I trembled. I was getting agitated that I only knew about half the people and homies here. They're all young boys with no clue of what they've gotten themselves into. It's a shame they're too young to die but too proud to cry, I thought.

"Sooo... so... what are you guys going to do about it?" Irvine's baby's mother sniffled out. I turned to look at her. She caught my eyes and looked away. "They killed Irvine, so what are we going to do?"

The silence was palpable. Even the birds seem to be silent, avoiding the spotlight. I wished for them to chirp, fly around, or do something so we could be distracted from this uncomfortable silence.

People avoided making eye contact. They hid their eyes by staring at the ground, the heap of flowers, their shoes, etc. If eye contact were made, it was by accident and was quickly released. No greater way of exposing your shame then by letting people capture the truth in your eyes.

For some bizarre reasons, I began to think of a movie where a group of soldiers were pinned down in their foxhole. They looked at each other with the same fear and uncertainty. I see now in the eyes of my homeboys. Then all of a sudden, one soldier stood up and said, "We must charge or stay here like cowards." He ran out of the foxhole toward his enemy only to be gunned down. Some of the soldiers thought he was brave while others thought he was a fool.

"Samantha, you don't have to worry about it. We know what we have to do!" My words came out sharply. She stopped her sniffling. She now had her fool. My homeboys eyes turned toward me, waiting for more words. I couldn't stand their questioning eyes looking at me for answers. I don't have any answers. I wanted to shout: I'm just like you, lost in this foolish game!

My mind was loud and I needed to search for someone who related to the way I felt. I turned to Little T. His eyes were down. He looked sickly, wobbling in the cool breeze. At that precise moment I regretted dragging him here. He seemed to be in a world of his own. He had his own demons to fight. I knew he would never make it out of that foxhole.

I searched for Hieu and found him squeezed between K and P. He was in a trance, staring at the display of flowers. He had on designer clothes to go with his $900 TAG Heuer watch. Hieu drove a new B.M.W. He had bended fate, willing it to release him from his truculent past. Making no excuses, he fought to better himself. He, too, I knew would not leave the foxhole. I began to feel even lonelier. The rope that had bound us youthful silly boys together was beginning to thin. In time would be no more. We were once young and invincible, but time had taken away our vanity and left us with nothing but memories!

"Silly Batman, why are you always holding onto the past?" I asked myself.

"This is bullshit!' I said.

A moment passed, nothing else was said. My homebody released me and I walked away, never to see most of them again.

A couple of weeks after Irvine's funeral, three of my homeboys and I went to visit his gravesite. The mounds of flowers were gone, except for a bundle of white lilies in a copper vase in the ground. We knew his mother and little sister visited him weekly.

The homies bent down and put a fresh bundle of lilies next to the ones his sister and mother brought (Irvine's favorite flowers). Another homeboy lights a Marlboro and stuck it next to the vase. We all spoke to him silently. After a long moment, we made our way to my homeboy's Danny's resting place, not far away. His father was there. My homeboys had told me he comes often after work, and he won't even allow the groundskeeper to mow the grass around where his son rests. He wanted to do it himself.

We came and bowed our heads; he nodded back at us in welcome. I could see around his son's resting place, the grass was freshly cut, neatly lined even. A used red push-mower sat idly a couple of steps away.

"I was going to go over and clean around your friend's place later." He motioned with his head toward Irvine's place.

We all thanked him.

"My wife should be coming to the states soon. If she runs into you boys and asks what happened to her son, please tell her he had died in a car accident coming home from school. He's her only child and she is very proud of him."

The way he asked sounded like a desperate plea for us to understand the pain it would cause his wife to know her boy was gunned down.

My heart was heavy thinking of his, and his wife's, pain. I looked at my homeboy's father and I saw more than just a tired old man. I saw a father who had done all he could to give his son a fair opportunity to succeed in this country. An opportunity we took away from both of them.

At that moment tears wanted to burst out of my eyes. I wanted to cry for him and his wife—for they will never have someone to care for them in their older years, and no grandchildren to play with or hug. I wanted to reach over and hug him; he would've probably thought I was crazy.

K bent down and put a bundle of flowers over my homeboy's marble plaque. Danny's father squatted down and rearranged the bundle, making sure that nothing blocked his son's handsome face and the three words underneath: A Loving Son.

—*Tuan "Mike" Doan*

Be Still

The heavy metal door rattled as the mechanical chain pulled it open. The loud noise was like a speaker announcing to those inside of a new arrival. I straightened my back, puffed out my chest. My face changed, masking my nervousness. With an uneasy step, I entered the pod, looking like a lost confused boy who had walked into a classroom full of strangers on his first day at a new school. Their eyes, cold, stared from behind the narrow Plexiglas window of their cells. They pierced into me like curious predators wondering who I am, friend or foe, and why I am here. My eyes met theirs, but only for a split second. I gave each a polite nod to acknowledge them as two correctional officers escorted me down the hall to the opened cell at the far end.

At the sight of the COs, a wild-eyed inmate began to shout out a litany of complaints and accusations. "You are holding my mail. I know it. Don't play games with me. You assholes turned down the pressure on my sink. I know it. There's no hot water. So that's how you guys want to play, huh? Well suckers, I wrote to the President of the U.S. of A." He dragged out the letter. "He's going to send his people down here to check you fools. Watch! They're gonna come... FBI succa. The badges is gonna shine all up ya faces." He went on and on with his mindless statements, sounding more and more like a J-cat (crazy). The CO's ignored him. So did I.

My heart raced as I entered my 6 by 8 foot cell that felt like a concrete tomb, no bigger than the bathroom of an average size home. The heavy door closed behind me, locking me inside this gray enclosed tomb, with a loud clang. I began to feel claustrophobic, drowned in the emptiness of the tiny cell.

I took in a needed breath and let out a calming sigh, hoping it would slow the anxieties that had begun to sweep over me.

"You'll get used to it. Things will get better," I tried comforting myself, but the feeling of despair and loneliness wouldn't allow comforting words to register in my mind. It felt as though there was a tug of war being fought between my analytical mind and my loud emotions. Each had its reason that the other stubbornly refused to accept. I felt tired, mentally drained. All I wanted was to lie down and sleep, to forget about this place, forget that I once again had been herded like cattle to a new farm.

I lazily walked over to the metal locker and removed the things I'd been holding from a plastic bag: a small plastic spoon, a roll of toilet paper, half a bar of soap, a two-inch toothbrush, and a paper cup with tooth powder sitting at the bottom. I laid everything neatly inside the locker then turned around to my concrete bed where an old worn mattress laid on top. It's insides spilled loosely out of the holes some inmate had tried desperately to patch up.

I removed one of the two clean, but just as worn, sheets lying on top of the mattress and hastily made my bed. I fell onto the bed, pulling the extra sheet over my head. I closed my eyes, pretending I was home in my comfortable bed with mom in the kitchen preparing a wonderful thanksgiving meal, the turkey perfectly glazed with my mom's secret sauce, its juicy aroma filling every room of the house. My stomach growled at the thought. I pushed the thought aside, not further teasing my empty stomach, and tried to sleep. But sleep was impossible on the thin lumpy mattress.

I tossed and turned trying desperately to find a decent spot, which couldn't be done. I curled into a fetal position, my hands tucked between my legs, cocooned underneath my sheet, listening to the wheezing vent blowing out cold air. The air so cold my teeth chattered and my body shivered uncontrollably in my white boxers and t-shirt.

Unable to sleep, I got up. I wrapped the sheet around my shoulder and paced the room, taking five quick steps, spinning around, and marching back. Back and forth I went, trying to keep warm with the repetitious movement to nowhere.

Boredom began to toy with my restless mind, forcing me to find ways to entertain myself. My eyes scanned the room, reading graffiti that inmates had written or scratches on walls, locker and door. Most of the graffiti was gang related, proudly displaying their alias and neighborhoods. But some were private thoughts. "Jenny, I love you" was printed neatly in pencil on the wall. The writer of the message remained anonymous, too ashamed of his foolish moment of amorousness to take claim. An innocent display of affection in a hostile environment could be perceived as a sign of weakness. "Too young to die, too proud to cry," was lazily scribbled on the side of the locker by Mr. Smurf. "John 3:16" was etched into the door.

After I was bored reading graffiti, I found new ways to entertain myself. I began to look for small holes and cracks in the walls. Two holes and a long crack in the middle became Mickey Mouse. But on further and careful inspection, I declared it to be Dumbo with his big ears and long nose. And on I went giving each notable combination of cracks and holes an identity. But after awhile, this too no longer entertained my quickly bored mind. And in no time, boredom was like a leaking faucet, so palpable in its tiny endless drops.

Unanswered questions about this place raced through my mind. Maybe I should ask my neighbor, I suggested to myself. No, I shouldn't. He didn't look too friendly standing behind the thick Plexiglas window, eyeing me with his tattooed chest like a billboard proudly advertising his neighborhood in big black letters. He might be another J-cat. But maybe he might not be, I painfully debated with myself. With dreaded heart, I hesitantly stepped onto the toilet, but shyly jumped back down. Go ahead, talk to him, the voice inside of me encouraged. Reluctantly, I stepped back onto the toilet, my face pressed close to the vent. "Excuse me neighbor," I called out above the wheezing vent, keeping the tone in my voice level.

"What's up?" a voice rang out from the other side. I could hear a foot climbing on top of the stainless steel toilet on the other side.

I politely told him my name, my ethnicity, and why I was here. He in turn did the same, with pleasantness in his voice that made my heart smile.

He gave me a succinct rundown of the program: "Shower every other day for five minutes, except Wednesday; laundry once a week on Thursday; no yard, no book—don't bother to ask. Make sure you ask for two blankets and a towel after dinner—that you could ask for."

I was given a heads up not to entertain the inmate who had shouted out at the COs with conversation. "He's a crazy," my neighbor warned. I already figured he was. "That dude's been in here for over two years. They said he attacked a CO who was talking shit to him." He was cool the first year, but now... man, he yelled and talked shit to everyone. They tried forcing him to take his pill but he refused."

After answering the rest of my inquiries, my neighbor kindly asked if I wanted to check out a book. "Yeah, of course," I wanted to shout. A book to me in a place where the only form of entertainment was staring at the walls or daydreaming was priceless. I would even trade my breakfast for a book. If it's a really good book, I'll even throw in my sack lunch. "Yeah, if you could spare one," I coolly replied.

A minute later, a fishing line torn from a sheet with a mustard pack tied to the end slid in front of my door. "Go ahead and pull two times on the line," he instructed. I stuck my fingers underneath the bottom crack and pulled on the line, and brought in a book split in half to fit underneath my door. I couldn't believe it. A western! My favorite. A giddy smile spread over my face. The book he loaned was clenched tightly in my hand.

The days, weeks, and months that followed our first meeting were quite interesting. The two of us, once complete strangers, separated by a thick wall that made us feel like we were a continent apart, now quickly bonded. This forged into an endearing friendship by the loneliness and boredom of this miserable place.

We spent our days passing time by working out. At night we stood on our toilet, our faces pressed inches from the vent so we could hear each other over the wheezing sound. Our faces ached from the cold air, but we didn't mind. We were just glad to be entertained by each other's stories about ourselves, our family, our girlfriend, our ex's, our hopes and our dreams.

We were two men from different cultures and different upbringing, but when we shared about our family, our shame and guilt were tangible to the other. We described how sad it was we had let our families down, especially our mothers, to whose endless love and encouragement we had failed to listen.

We talked about letting go of our past and starting anew, never forgetting our bad choices, but also never letting them define who we are or who we desire to become: better human beings.

Twice a week, mostly on weekends, we declared an hour of karaoke night. That hour we sang whatever we wanted. Madonna's "Like a Virgin" got a little play. And mostly due to my unyielding encouragement, my somewhat shy neighbor would always kick it off. He sang off-key and often with missing lyrics. I would grin and painfully hold back the laughter that was itching to burst through my throat. I was always kind in giving him praise, even suggesting he could go on American Idol and possibly win. He laughed. I laughed.

When it was my turn, I sang with all my passion and soul as though I was singing in front of thousands, not just one. And, no matter how dreadful my singing was, my neighbor was quick to shower me with compliments. I smiled at his kind words, but knew quite well that, on the other side of the wall, a big grin was spreading over his face.

Time flew as we continued to find new ways to entertain ourselves in the hole. Our corny jokes were so lame we had to laugh. But everything changes, and time seemed to be at a standstill for me the day he got word he was transferring. We said our goodbyes, wishing each other a safe and better journey in life. That night again I felt alone and overwhelmed with the silence, except for the wheezing vent. I laid on my bed and read the last chapter of the book I had been saving just for a moment like this. I put it down beside me after I had finished reading it, quite upset at myself for reading it so fast. My eyes stared blankly into the room. My mind zoned out with thoughts of lonely days ahead.

I thought about my neighbor and one of the stories he had shared. A thin smile spread over my face. "Man, when I was young, every time I got in trouble and my mom spanked me, I would wail and cry, pretending it hurt. She would feel guilty and stop." He laughed a hearty laughter full of boyish innocence. "Man, this always worked," he declared pertly, paused, and then added with a profound sincerity: "Man, I love her."

My eyes, lost in a trance, stared at the dim glow from the yellow light above my sink. A barely legible writing above the sink caught my eyes. I wondered how I'd missed it. I squinted my eyes, too lazy to get up, and read it. I read it again, slowly. I closed my eyes, allowing the words to sink into my heart. My feeling of despair and loneliness began to lift from my heart, and in its place were feelings of gratitude and appreciation. My mind, for the first time since I've been here, became still.

I opened my eyes and looked around at my surroundings, grateful to have a roof over my head, clothes to wear, and three meals a day. I spoke softly the words on the wall, filling the empty silence with its touching message: "I complained because I have no shoes, then I met a man who had no feet."

Thy soul shall find itself alone
'Mid dark thoughts of the gray tombstone—
Not one of the crowd to pry
Into thine hour of secrecy.
Be silent in that solitude,
Which is not loneliness, for then
The spirit of the dead who stood
In life before thee, on their will
Shall overshadow thee:
Be still.

[From the book Gemini Man]

—Tuan "Mike" Doan

Another Wounded Soul

Courage, Love, Friendship, Compassion and Empathy... Lift us above the simple beasts and define humanity.

Once or twice a year, thirty to forty men from around the world, and across the United States, come together for a four-day training inside New Folsom Prison. These men are selected out of a pool of hundreds of men. Those who are selected, but not prepared for the training, will be interviewed, processed, and weeded out by inmates and outside facilitators. This process is to ensure that each man knows exactly what he is doing, because he and another man will be in charge of guiding, facilitating, and caring for the man who's going through the training.

Inmates and outside facilitators try their best to be free from any emotional baggage during the training so they can focus their energy into helping those who are emotionally wounded. However, sometimes things don't always go as planned and facilitators at times get triggered by the work of others; in doing so, they also need support.

One of our facilitators, Dan, who stood about 6'2" and weighed close to 230 pounds, had never shied away from confrontation, especially if he believed he was in the right. However, his roommate Tom was the total opposite. Tom always avoided confrontation regardless of if he was right. He was known as a gentle and kind person.

Both men had hoped to get a good night sleep so they would be fresh and ready the next morning for the training. Their sleep was constantly interrupted by a bunch of college students who were playing loud music and making lots of noise. They tried their best not to let the noise bother them. Unfortunately, Dan's mood had gone from being annoyed to frustrated, and finally to anger.

Dan had had enough and decided to go and comfort these kids.

Tom knew he could not let Dan go out there alone in a confrontational state of mind, so he decided to come along just in case something went wrong. As the both of them were about to walk out of the door, Dan had an epiphany and immediately turned to Tom and said, "What am I doing? I'm going to prison tomorrow!" Tom was extremely relieved and knew exactly what Dan meant. Confronting these kids could make things even worse; besides, their commitment to the men in blue (inmates) was more important and worthwhile. Dan and Tom didn't sleep well that night, but I was sure glad to see them the next morning with a story to share.

Every morning, the men gathered together by the prison gate around 8, so they could all be let in at once. As they waited, curious COs (correctional officers) at times would ask, "Why do they choose to come in here?" Most COs after hearing a lucid explanation by one of the facilitators, became more understanding of what they were trying to do. However, once in a while, they came upon a hostile CO who questioned the validity of what they're doing. One CO asked, "Why do you guys waste your time coming in here when there are lots of people out there who you could help?"

Most of the men avoid answering those types of questions, fearing what they might say could further agitate the CO, which could bring unnecessary harassment. But a few men took their chances and tried to give their reason. One man's heartfelt reason was: "I came to help men who are wounded and who most of society consider incorrigible. I believed by healing these inmates' heart, their mind could then slowly discard all the negative thinking and let go of past pains."

As soon as the first man finished speaking, another man immediately voiced his opinion: "I should have been in prison for all the bad choices I made. And if I was in there, I would hope someone cared enough to come and show me a better way to deal with my emotional pains so I would stop hurting others and myself."

On another day a similar question was asked. And to everyone's surprise, the most shy and introverted man in the group managed the courage to speak up. John nervously said, "Officer, I came to this prison not to help those inmates, but to ask these inmates for their help. I truly believed that these inmate facilitators really care about helping me and other inmates. They don't seek out recognition, accolades, or money for what they do. They do it for the pure pleasure of seeing someone happy." His answer caught the CO by surprise because the CO had always thought that these men came to help inmates and never once did he consider that inmates were capable of helping these free men.

After my second day of training, as I stood by the chapel door, I noticed that the most hated CO on the yard was walking toward me. He had a reputation for messing with inmates in the program who he didn't like. Constantly searching their cell, throwing personal property all over the floor, including food, clothes, appliances, hygiene, etc. He made sure that the cell resembled the destruction made by a tornado, sometimes locking inmates in isolation with little or no justifications.

His truculent demeanor had caused him to be stabbed and beaten numerous times by inmates, which only further increased his resolve to get tougher.

Now as he was coming toward me, I began to wonder, "Have I done something wrong?" I was uneasy when he came and stood next to me. After close to a minute of standing there, not saying a word, he turned his head toward me and nonchalantly asked, "Why are these guys coming in here for? You and I both know they can't change anybody in here. You inmates are too tough to change." I wasn't sure if he had thrown the last comment out to get a response or reaction from me.

I contemplated if I should entertain his question and comment. I decided the best thing to do was to be polite and give a concise response, which turned to be longer than what I had expected.

I started off by letting him know how many sacrifices these men had made just to be here. Some men came as far away as England, Ireland, South Africa, Australia, and all over the U.S. Most flew but some drove half a day to be here. They then had to spend their own money for food and lodging.

These men came with a purpose: to help heal wounds and mend broken hearts. Furthermore, to show men a better way to deal with frustration and anger, and not allow their emotions to manifest into violence; to show compassion and love in an environment that often breeds hatred and mistrust.

I went on and told him that all religions and beliefs are welcome in this group. There are Christians, Muslims, Buddhists, Indian medicine men, atheists, and many others. These men came together knowing that no matter what their beliefs are, as human beings each man is tangible to his own suffering, and by recognizing their own pains, they are able to empathize and reach out to help others in pain, in the process healing their own wounds.

As I finished sharing why these men came, a question came to me, and I was curious of what his response would be. I went ahead and asked. "What do you think about the way some of these men dressed?" For a moment he had a puzzled expression on his face, which in turn made me feel silly for asking. After a few seconds of uncomfortable silence, which felt like minutes, I decided to rephrase my question: "What is your opinion of some of the men just by the way they dress?" I wasn't sure if I had rephrased my question any different but the puzzled look on his face slowly disappeared, which was reassuring. After a few seconds of deliberation he gave his response, "I've been working here for over 20 years and I've seen many volunteers coming in here dressed real sharp, but I noticed a few men in your group dressed a little too casual. Some wearing flip-flops, shoes with no socks, and unkempt hair. A few even looked like ex-cons. But for me to judge them deeper just by the clothes they wore is unreasonable. I admired these men for all the time and money they invested in you guys, because I surely wouldn't volunteer four days, from 8 in the morning until 6 or 7 at night. I'd rather be with my family and loved ones."

His answer had completely caught me off guard. I expected him to be judgmental and mean. He turned out to be quite understanding of the volunteers, and his frankness and honest opinion made me somewhat admire him.

I stood there feeling foolish and guilty for trying to get this CO to reaffirm what my judgment of him was.

I had always thought that most staff misjudged some of the free men because of their shabby clothes, like I once had. Thinking some of the men were financially poor, probably ex-drug addicts or alcoholics with no purpose in life but to come into prison to share stories of how they got their life together.

I know even though he hadn't judged these volunteers' character or financial situation, I still wanted to share some of their professions with him. I asked if he wanted to know what some of these men did outside of this prison. He hesitated for a second then said "sure." I told him these men were lawyers, doctors, accountants, business men, military officers (retired sergeants, captains, colonels), retired correctional officers, professors (some with prestigious universities), writers (one was on the New York Times best sellers' list), a movie director (who directed "Hoop Dreams"), poets, prison chaplains, students, and many other honorable professions.

After I finished, I could see a hint of surprise and respect in his eyes. I went on and let him know I realized these men didn't come to impress me or anybody with their expensive clothes or how big their account was—they came to show me how big was their heart.

I wanted to say something else, but I saw another CO beginning to pat inmates down so they could go inside the chapel. I politely excused myself and headed toward the chapel door.

As I walked away, I felt a little sad, knowing that I was able to walk inside a place where I have people to help me deal with my pain. But the CO who had spent all that time talking about love, compassion, and emotional healing was still standing there carrying his own burden. For that moment, I didn't care if he was wearing a green jumpsuit and I was in my prison blue. I somehow felt this tangible connection to another wounded soul.

I learned a lot that day. Always keep my heart open and allow my compassion and love to guide my judgment of others.

After that day, the same CO and I spoke a few more times. Each time I noticed the wall he had enclosed around his heart many years ago was slowly being removed, one brick at a time.

Now sometimes I hear him joking around with inmates.

P.S.: I truly believe God has blessed every person with a fire that burns inside his or her heart. It's up to us to remove all the filth, dirt, and calluses we have piled over our heart for so many years. God's love shines in each one of us; it's up to us how bright we want it to shine.

Thanks to all the men and women who spent countless hours volunteering in juvenile hall, county jail, and prison—a special thanks to all the inmate facilitators and volunteers at New Folsom Prison. Your work and compassion are changing lives.

—*Tuan "Mike" Doan*

A Little Girl

In prison, inmates do not really look forward to many things. Birthdays, holidays, and anniversaries become part of this blur as each and every day are mashed into the same monotonous day. Like what my last cellie said, "Everyday is Halloween, everyday is my birthday. It's all the same old shit day in and day out." However, there are days when we begin to feel somewhat human again, rather than just a number. Those are visits.

The outcome of a visit is crucial to the mental and emotional state of mind for many inmates. The way one's visit goes can dictate one's mental predicament until the next one. If it goes well, then more power to you. If not, then may God have mercy on you.

Fortunately, my visits have been wonderful, graced by a little girl named Kaylyn.

I woke up, eyes wide-open, early Saturday morning. It was still dark outside as the sun just barely began to caress the horizon. I couldn't go back to sleep as the adrenaline rushed into my veins with a million thoughts racing into my mind. I will finally see my family today after a year of waiting.

My roommate was still asleep recovering from the night before. The remnant of last night was evident as the stale smell of alcohol lurked in the air. I didn't mind though. I just laid there imagining what I'd say to my family, how I'd love and miss them.

My roommate finally awoke from his deep sleep with a hangover, which prompted me to rush to the sink and brush my teeth. I then proceeded to cut my hair with a clipper. Going over it several times to make sure I had not missed a hair. Afterwards I shaved my face with a razor. Once again. Going over it several times. It had to be perfect. I wanted to look good for my family.

Finally, I removed my prison blue shirt and pants from underneath my mattress, which I had neatly folded and left there until my visit. They were creased to precision as if someone had just ironed it.

Eight o'clock came and I became excited as the inmates' names were called for visits. Some of those who got visits looked jubilant. While others carried the same stone countenance they carried on a daily basis.

Three hours had passed and people began coming back from their visits. All my thoughts of happiness were replaced with anxiety and despair. What's going on? Is my family okay? Did they get into an accident, or had they simply forgot to come? Fear gripped me at the last thought.

Thirty minutes later I heard my name called for a visit. I quickly got dressed and began repeatedly flashing my lights to let the correctional officer know I was ready. But after close to thirty minutes, panic set in when they still didn't let me out. As I stood there I contemplated saying these words, "You bastards are holding up my visit!" As soon as the door slid open, I rushed outside not bothering to let my roommate know where I was going.

I hurried across the prison yard; friends and acquaintances waved and wished me a wonderful visit. No time to talk, I waved and hurried on.

I got to the outer visiting checkpoint and was stripped and searched by a slow meticulous guard. I wanted to yell, "Come on man, hurry up," but I decided to exercise my dwindling patience. I reminded myself that my hassles were nothing compared to what my family had gone through. I imagined them driving all night for nine hours or more, then having to wait in line for hours to be processed through. Standing outside with little or no protection from the elements, such as rain, wind, and the hot sun. Getting through in under an hour is considered a blessing.

If they wore clothes that were not acceptable, such as blue jeans, white or blue shirts, bras with metal lining, skirts or blouses two inches above the knee, etc., they are given an opportunity to rummage through the used clothes that is provided by charity.

Then they are told to line up in the back again. Once they made it inside, they are inspected for contraband, making them feel as though they were criminals themselves. Thinking of their sacrifices put me in a calm state of mind.

After the guard finished inspecting me, I walked into the visiting room, began scanning for my family, but wasn't able to pick them out. I finally met my mother's eyes and at once was relieved. The feeling of joy took over.

My mother was standing there looking tired, but still had her beautiful smile when I approached. I stopped in my track, not because I was arrested by her presence, but rather by the fact that I didn't know how to greet her. My rigid culture has always preached it was not right to show affection or hug one's family after a certain age, for men at least.

At that instant, I thought it was crazy to obey such tradition and decided to relinquish my strict upbringing and do what I felt right. I opened my arms and gave her a big hug. She paused for a second before returning the display of affection emitting tears of joy. I was surprised when she held me in her embrace longer than I expected. At that very moment, I felt this undeniable love from my mother and she in turn confirmed that no matter what happens, I would always be her son.

For a second, I was so consumed with my mother's love that I almost forgot to greet my older sister and younger brothers. The surprised looks on their faces when my mother shown such emotions was evident. By the wetness in their eyes, I could tell they were happy for me.

I sat down on the dull cushioned chair adjacent to my mother and inquired how she was doing. The hard part was getting my mother to talk about herself. She is too consumed about helping others, paying little attention to herself. What little she shared meant so much to me.

While my sister Katie was asking me questions about prison life, I noticed a crib to her side. This must be my newborn niece. I looked inside and saw this beautiful angelic face. She stared intensely at me with her big beautiful brown eyes. It looked as if she didn't have a care in the world. All she was focused on was sucking her thumb and this stranger staring at her.

I couldn't resist any longer. I had to pick her up. I lifted her up and cradled her in my left arm, and with my right hand I fed her with her star-covered baby bottle. With her free hand she held onto my shirt and snuggled in my arm. For a moment she made me forget I was in prison. I felt peace and joy just holding her.

Kaylyn didn't come again until the following year. By then she was about one and a half. She could barely walk, but somehow managed to stand up on her own. She looked like a baby doll, wobbling back and forth every time she stood up. She never cried or frowned whenever she fell.

I couldn't help but take her around and show her off to my friends and their families. My friends thought she was adorable. They asked if they could hold her. Knowing that some of my friends haven't held a baby in years convinced me to let them hold her.

She seemed to be as comfortable in someone else's arms as she was in mine. Kaylyn enjoyed the attention she was receiving. Not saying much, Kaylyn would giggle and laugh when people made faces or funny noises.

Close to a year passed of not seeing my family, especially Kaylyn. I became anxious, always asking my family when the next time I could see my niece again.

She finally came, but the prison at the time was going through major turmoil. Tensions ran high as the prison was inundated with racial riots and staff assaults. The occurrences had brought down a gloomy environment among all its residents and staff. It was as though the walls had become grayer. As one old convict put, "In prison one's program or even one's life can be changed in a heartbeat."

Kaylyn had grown. She was almost three years old by then. She looked so adorable in her star-spangled white and pink sweats. She even had pretty little pink shoes to match her outfit.

I could see her beaming with joy bouncing behind the two-foot visiting table, pretending to hide from me. I was so happy to see her, but a little worried that she might not remember me.

My fear melted away when she rushed over to give me a hug. "Who's your favorite uncle?" I asked.

"Yo ar, unca Tuan!" she said in her sweet baby voice. The only word that was lucid was my name. I lifted her up as far as my hands could reach and spun in a circle. She laughed and giggled uncontrollably. "Mo unca Tuan!" Just like the last time she came, I took her around and introduced Kaylyn to some of my friends that had been asking for her. Kaylyn would cross her arms and bow her head like she had been taught. She attempted to repeat what I just said, but instead she mumbled, "Ha ar yuu?"

After all the introductions, I brought her back to our table. My family and I began conversing. We had lots to talk about. While we were deep in our conversation not paying attention to Kaylyn, she wandered off.

Panic gripped my heart. I knew we were in a safe area, but this is still prison. Due to the current situation on the yard I wasn't sure if she would be well-received by other inmates.

We began scanning the room. Our worries were quickly laid to rest when we saw her playing with a black family. She wasn't actually playing but rather stacking the chess pieces. We could see that the family was enamored with her.

"Tuan, go get your niece—she's interrupting other people's visits," my sister pleaded.

I went over and apologized, for I did not know what she was up to. To my surprise, the family implored that she's nothing but a joy. They were hoping she could stay a little longer.

The inmate explained, "Man, your niece is so cool. She kicked it with us like she is our folks. She doesn't seem to mind about my tattoo, or the fact we have different color skins."

After taking her away from the reluctant family, I found her again a few minutes later walking in between a black couple holding hands. She walked around the visiting room as though they were her parents. She giggled and laughed when they lifted her up. I was amazed that Kaylyn could gravitate toward a complete stranger. She didn't seem to have a care in the world.

My sister Katie was getting a little frustrated with Kaylyn for wandering off again. I tried to reassure her that nothing was going to happen to Kaylyn. I explained that some inmates haven't seen their children in years and others don't have children. They treated Kaylyn as their own baby. But that didn't ease her worries or frustrations with Kaylyn.

Katie tried to wave Kaylyn over, but Kaylyn pretended not to see or hear her mother. That only further upset her mom.

My sister once again finally got Kaylyn's attention and gave her the coldest stare and waved her over. Kaylyn reluctantly let go of their hands and mumbled something to them. I could tell by the look on Kaylyn's face that she was afraid of her mother.

The couple escorted Kaylyn over and praised Kaylyn for being such a sweet and well-behaved girl. They even joked about adopting and bringing her home. My sister managed a faint smile after hearing their comments. After seeing her mom smile, Kaylyn began to relax, believing that she was off the hook.

Not long after receiving a stern lecture from her mom, we realized that Kaylyn had wandered off again. This time we had found her talking to this Caucasian inmate. This inmate shook my mom because he didn't look like an ordinary guy. Kaylyn was talking to a guy who stood 6'8" and weighed close to 300 pounds. He had muscles bulging out of his shirt. He could have easily been a football player but instead was serving a life sentence for murder. Fortunately, he was a friend of mine. I tried to reassure my family that my friend Tom was harmless, but it didn't ease their worries one bit.

"Go get your niece before she upsets someone or gets herself into trouble," my sister once again pleaded.

I walked over to where Kaylyn was and I could hear her and Tom talking about the candies in her hand. I'm pretty sure Tom didn't understand what Kaylyn was saying, but he pretended to converse with her anyway. I told Tom I needed to take her back before her mom gets mad.

When I got Kaylyn back to the table, my mom discovered she had a dollar bill in her hand. The look of embarrassment was evident on my mom's face.

"See, I told you your niece was going to get herself into trouble," my sister angrily pointed out. My mom asked I bring Kaylyn back to Tom with the money and apologize.

Tom was talking to his girlfriend when he saw us coming. He motioned to his girlfriend to turn around and they both smiled. We got to their table and I asked Kaylyn to cross her hands and bow her head, which she did. I asked her to say sorry, but instead she mumbled something that I didn't understand. So I pointed to her hand and explained that the money belonged to my friend. Kaylyn somewhat understood what I was saying and tried to return the money she was holding in her left hand. But Tom refused to take the money. He would pull his hands away whenever she tried to put the money in his hand.

Kaylyn figured her plea wouldn't work and quickly turned to diplomacy by offering him a handful of melted M&Ms from her right hand. The M&Ms were so dilapidated they no longer resembled their former color or size. Though Tom was hesitant, he willingly took the M&Ms from her hand and pretended to eat them, causing Kaylyn to emit a giggle. He then raised his enormous hands and coaxed Kaylyn to give him a low five, which Kaylyn playfully obliged. She smacked her right hand, which had been holding the M&Ms, on top of Tom's giant hand. The melted M&Ms now glued to Tom's hand, causing him to make several faces and grunts. This only made Kaylyn laugh harder. Tom couldn't help but smile and laugh along at the sight of Kaylyn jumping up and down laughing. Watching them interact toward each other could cause one to believe they must be best friends.

Tom later explained he playfully tried to buy the M&Ms from Kaylyn. She had refused to sell them, but managed to walk away with his money anyway.

After visiting that day, one inmate wanted me to know that being with Kaylyn gave him hope of being a better father to his children when he gets out. Other inmates requested I bring her back as soon as possible. Kaylyn came back the next day, but she wasn't feeling well. She wasn't as outgoing as the day before. The whole day she wanted to be held by either her mom or her grand-mother.

At the end of our visit, she was walking up and ramp heading toward the exit. For some reason she stopped midway, looked back at me for a few seconds, and ran back down to give me a hug. She didn't seem to hear my family or the guard yelling at her to stop running. Maybe she did but chose not to listen.

Kaylyn held onto me as though she didn't want to let go. Neither did I. I guess we both knew we wouldn't see each other again until some time the next year.

P.S.: It's funny how we are constantly searching for happiness in things that do not make sense. We choose money, materialistic things, or a broken relationship, but none seem to make us hap-pier. Then you look at something as simple as a sweet little girl named Kaylyn, who through her innocence and color blindness managed to touch hearts and break down stereotypes.

It was by watching her I began to appreciate the time when things were simpler and we did not have a care in the world.

I believe there will always be that little boy or girl in us, wick-ering like a candle in the winds of change. All we have to do is keep it lit.

—*Tuan "Mike" Doan*

I Am a Man

His eyes closed, he rocked gently back and forth in his wooden rocker, taking in the cool breeze of an early spring morning. He could hear the gentle wind, laughing, toying with the leaves from an oak tree, blowing branches one way then another. Sparrows and finches chirped loudly with excitement, hopping from branch to branch, chasing away unwanted visitors from newly claimed territory. A bee buzzed around the old man. He was tempted to chase it away with his hand but decided to let it be and hope it will go on with its business and leave him alone. After a few seconds the bee flew away, probably to the flowers that had sprouted out from the once frozen ground.

The sound of nature full of life danced around him, relaxing his body and sending his silent thoughts back to the never forgotten past, forcing him to conjure images that had long ago been ingrained in the back of consciousness. He wished the images weren't there, but they were. He had resigned to the fact they would always be there, be part of him. He had tried pushing them back, way back, but stubbornly the images refused to obey and slowly drifted into his thoughts, dwelling in his mind until he could no longer resist their unwanted visits. And once again, he painfully gave in.

"You're just a monkey boy," the kid in his school had teased. "Go back to where you came from, monkey boy." "Monkey boy! Monkey boy!" they shouted in unison. Their taunting words coursed through his veins, on fire. These words inched closer to his heart, poisoning it with each painful breath he took. His tiny chest heaved heavily, begging for the cool air to fill his aching lungs and slow the pounding in his heart, which he was afraid would explode and kill him. Maybe it would be best if it did explode, he silently thought. That way he wouldn't be around for them to tease.

Dejected and alone, he painfully walked away. His feet began to move faster and faster, taking him further and further away from his tormentors. His feet pounded on the dirt path that led to his home. He quickly dashed inside, headed straight for the bathroom. Staring at himself in the mirror, he angrily brushed the shameful tears that had streaked down his face. He picked up a wooden brush and tried to straighten out his nappy hair, wishing it wasn't so nappy, for that's what the kids in school had called it. Frustrated that all his attempts were in vain, he took a clipper and shaved it all off. He looked at himself in the mirror. For a split second his chest was no longer crushing him. He took in an easy breath. No longer a nappy head. At that moment, he didn't' care if his mom would be disappointed by what he did. He had his reasons and she couldn't understand. They didn't make fun of her. They didn't laugh at and taunt her.

He knew his mom would try to comfort him. Like many other times she would speak with gentle encouragement, "Son, let Jesus guide your heart and let hope fill your mind." Her kind words, and unconditional love for him, only brushed at his heart. At that time, they hardly registered to his 7-year-old mind.

He wished he was no longer a boy but a man—a big strong man, so big no one would dare tease him. And if they did, he would send his fists into them with a grievance they would understand and remember. For it was his right to be a man.

The old man slowly opened his wise old eyes and they were wet. A tear had escaped the corner of his eyes and streaked down his face. He thought about his mom, how wise and loving she was to him and those around her. He wished he could go back in time and shake the youthful ignorance he had allowed to fill his heart with false pride, a foolish pride that had chained him down, refusing to let him become a good man like his mother had envisioned and prayed for. No! He was a fool who lost twenty good years of his life behind bars, a concrete tomb he had called home.

The old man sadly shook his pepper gray hair. He took a deep breath, let out a long sigh to gather himself before getting up. He strolled over to the garden. He bent down, his back like a crescent moon, and began pulling out weeds that had crept in around his flowers. In the short distance, he could see little Tim walking to school, his blonde hair lightly tossing in the wind. A good boy. Little Tim waved his hand at the old man. The old man straightened his body; once again he felt big and strong. He gave the little boy a warm smile and returned the wave.

—Tuan "Mike" Doan

A Silent Prayer

I was thirteen years old when I was arrested for driving a stolen vehicle. My male and female passengers were let go. I was then brought to juvenile hall where I was stripped naked and searched. My personal belongings were confiscated and I was issued dark blue pants and a t-shirt. I was allowed a five-minute phone call which I declined, then given a quick shower and sent to my cell. In there was a thin mattress, two sheets, and a blanket on top of a concrete bed. The room was filthy with spit and graffiti all over the walls and floor. The smell of urine permeated the cell.

I sat there stunned and upset. Just a few hours ago, I had the freedom and liberty to go anywhere and do anything I wanted. But now I was confined in this eight-by-ten-foot hellhole called a "cell." I climbed onto my unmade bed and fell asleep trying to escape from my reality.

The next morning, the realization of what I'd done and where I was finally set in. I felt so alone and ashamed. I had let down so many people, especially my mother who depends on me to set an example for my younger siblings.

For the next three days I was confined in my cell with nothing but time to stress and reflect on my mistakes. After three days of processing, I was finally placed in a regular unit and allowed two hours of dayroom each day. In those two hours I had the opportunity to take a shower, use the phone, or watch television. I looked forward to those two precious hours. It was a means for me to escape the melancholy in a cell.

A few times during dayroom, I was tempted to call my mom but decided that it was best for me not to burden her with expensive collect calls. Besides, she already had a difficult time taking care of six kids by herself in a foreign country. I wanted her to come and visit me or be at my court hearing, but there was no way I could ask.

One night during dayroom, a couple in their early-to-mid sixties entered our unit and headed toward the back room. My counselor announced they were holding Bible study for those wishing to attend. A few of the kids started making fun of the couple. "The Holy Rollers are here," one kid said. "Let's go see if they brought some cookies," another kid jovially joined in.

I waited to see if anybody would go, but there were no brave souls that dared face the teasing. I didn't want to go. I wanted to spend these precious two hours watching television. After a few minutes passed, I couldn't stand the thought of these two people sacrificing their time, which none of us seemed to appreciate.

I pushed my fear aside, got up, and walked toward the back room. I expected the teasing to begin. Instead, all I got were a few curious stares.

I went inside and sat on one of those chairs that were in the circle. I felt extremely nervous meeting these two people. I didn't know what they expected of me, and my shyness didn't help.

The man (who I will call Nick) introduced himself and his wife (who I'll call Jane) to me.

After the introduction, we all sat down and Nick began to explain why they were there. He and his wife had been coming every other week for Bible studies. Sometimes one or two kids would show up and other times no one came.

After a quick explanation of what they did, Nick asked, "Are you a Christian?"

I answered, "No sir, I am a Catholic." Nick smiled and explained that Catholics and Protestants are both Christians. He went on to explain that Christians believe in Jesus Christ as their life and savior.

"Have you ever studied the Bible?" Nick asked.

"Yes sir, I was taught about the Bible in my communion class," I answered.

"Do you pray?" Jane asked.

"Yes ma'am. My dad taught me how to say the rosary every night and how to give thanks before we eat," I said.

Jane wanted to start the Bible study since no one else was coming. She handed me a Bible and asked me to turn to the book of Matthew, chapter seven. I didn't know where Matthew was. She seemed to sense my lack of knowledge about the Bible and saved me the embarrassment by showing me what page it was on.

She began to read Matthew, chapter seven: "Judge not, that you be judged." And for the next thirty minutes Jane and Nick dissected every verse in Matthew, chapter seven. I honestly didn't understand some of what they were teaching and it didn't help that I failed to ask questions.

After the Bible study, Jane asked if I wanted to say a prayer. I had never said a prayer out loud or in front of anyone before. I wasn't sure how to say a proper prayer, so I just said "No."

Nick explained that when he and his wife prayed, they were actually talking to God. God is not only our father, but also our best friend. God forgives our sins if we ask. I was a little confused because I thought only a priest could ask God to forgive someone for their sins.

Nick asked if I wanted him to say a prayer for me.

"Yes sir, can you pray to God to take care of my mother and siblings? Also can you pray for my father to go to heaven?" I could hear Nick asking God to use me and to shine his blessings on me. While he continued to pray, all the worries and stress from that past week slowly went away. I felt at peace and decided to say a "sillent prayer" for myself. "Praise God, let my mom come and see me." At that moment I felt selfish and ashamed; I was a sinner and didn't deserve my prayer to be answered. I tried to push my guilt aside and reminded myself of what Nick said earlier: "God is not only your father but also your friend, and it's all right to talk to him."

After we finished our prayer, Nick and Jane had to leave. Before they left, they each gave me a big hug and asked if I would come back again. I briefly hesitated but responded, "Yes."

That weekend as I sat in the dayroom, watched television, and observed other kids whose parents were visiting, I happened to see someone walking by my unit resembling my mother. I immediately turned to the kid sitting next to me and said, "She looks like my mom."

"She couldn't be because she is going over to the next unit," he said. I knew he was right, but for a moment I was happy.

A couple minutes passed and the same lady walked by the front of our unit. Once again I thought she looked like my mom, and after a longer look I realized she was my mom. I went to my counselor and told him I just saw my mom walk by. He quickly opened the door and waved my mom in.

She came inside and I could see the tired but happy look on her face. There were no hugs or handshakes. I was taught that affection is reserved only for young children. I felt too old to give my mom a hug, and a handshake seemed too formal and disrespectful.

We just sat across from each other on the picnic table in the back of the unit. Neither one of us knew what to say. I was ashamed for letting her down, and she blamed herself for me being in here.

I asked her how she knew I was here. She explained that a few nights ago, she couldn't sleep. She was tossing and turning all night worried that something had happened to me since I hadn't called home. She then asked my sister to call around to find me. My sister got information that I was being detained at juvenile hall.

My mom asked a friend to drive her to see me because she was unable to speak English and didn't know her way around town. They mistakenly drove three hours to juvenile camp. At arrival, they were told I was at juvenile hall, not camp. Hours later, they finally arrived. Again, my mother got lost because she couldn't understand the directions given to her. They handed her a piece of paper and she went to where they pointed.

After hearing what my mom had gone through, I fought to keep my tears from coming down. Inside, I was dying. I couldn't stand seeing her in so much pain because of me.

"Can I bring you some food and a blanket the next time I come?" she pleaded.

"Mom, they won't allow you to bring anything. Besides, I have everything I need already."

I shared with her about the Bible study and my private prayer that I gave a few days ago. She was happy that I had attended Bible study because she had also been praying for me.

Our visit was cut short because my mother had arrived really late. But it didn't matter because my "silent prayer" was already answered.

A few days after my visit, my counselor approached me to let me know I could go home tomorrow if I agreed to do forty-five days of community service. I happily agreed. That was the last time I saw Nick and Jane, but they left me with a gift I'd never forget.

Looking back, it was a very long time ago when two amazing people taught me the power of prayer. They taught me that God is not only my father but also my friend. Since then, I have carried Jesus in my heart wherever I've gone—Jesus has guided me through so many obstacles.

Since my meeting with Nick and Jane, God has continued to send me his "angels" in the form of volunteers who have shown nothing but compassion and love, even to a sinner like me.

"Everyone has different ways of connecting to God. We have different beliefs; we speak different languages and use different words. But if there is any rule at all concerning prayer, it is that however you pray, you must put forth an effort for your prayer to be answered." [Rabbi Irwin Katsof]

—Tuan "Mike" Doan

Have You Forgiven Yourself?

I have not forgiven myself. I don't know how. How do you forgive yourself for something you cannot change? How do you forgive yourself for harm you've caused to family members who are dead and gone?

My incarceration caused a rift between my grandmother and my mom. In 1984, my mom made me move to California even though I did not want to move. I had been living with my grandmother in Kentucky for years. My grandmother told my mom I could continue to live with her, but my mom insisted. This changed the course of my entire life.

My grandma blamed my mom for this. She blamed her for me joining a gang. She blamed her for me being shot and my subsequent incarceration.

My grandma passed away in 2001, six months after my granddad passed away. My granddad passed away a year after my dad passed away. Momma passed away in 2006, ten years after I was incarcerated.

I will never be able to make things right with them. Any of them. Or say the things I never got to say.

The worst part is, after depending on these beautiful people all of my life as a child, they were never able to depend on me as a man. As an adult.

My grandparents put up their house to pay an attorney who promised my family he would negotiate a plea significantly better than the 19 years the D.A. had been offering, a year and a half prior to being paid to come on as my attorney of record. Six months later, he convinced me my best option was to plead to a 30-year term.

He lied. He told my family if he could not negotiate a better plea he would give back half of the payment. He did not. He gave back less than 20 percent. In the end, my lineage no longer has my grandparents' home in our family. My family always believed I would be the one to elevate my family. I brought my family down. How do you forgive yourself for that?

The absolute worst was losing my mom to cancer. This beautiful lady had always been there for me each, including every time I was admitted to the hospital as an infant for severe asthma attacks. This lady was there when a car hit me. This lady showed up every single time I had a seizure as a result of being hit by this car. This lady was there at the hospital when I was shot and almost died. Six months later, when the family drove back to Kentucky from California to visit family, and my dad fell asleep behind the wheel, everyone walked away but me. Momma held my hand while my head was stapled; she stayed next to my hospital bed for three days while I was in a coma. This lady flew into town for three days for my preliminary hearing; she cried for three days except while she was in the courtroom where she sat stoic with a smile every time I looked her way. She died in a hospital by herself. When she needed me I wasn't there. How can I forgive myself for that?

I grew up without my father. The dad referred to above is my little sister's dad, my step-dad. The first time I ever talked to my biological father in life, I was 18 years old. I promised my son's mom and myself I would never leave my children that way. I would never abandon my children.

I was arrested Feb. 18th, 1996. This was five days before my oldest son's first birthday. His mom, my wife, was pregnant. She gave birth the same day, officially making my sons almost twins who were born one year, one hour, and 10 minutes apart, in the exact same hospital room.

My oldest son was my best bud. I took this little guy everywhere. He used to sleep on my chest and dance on the front seat of my lowrider car, and play with the hydraulics. Then one day I vanished. I didn't see him again for five years. After this I didn't see him again until he was 20.

My youngest son didn't know me and was distant from me. I remember in 1999 his mom telling him, "Come here, your dad wants to speak with you on the phone.

He responded, "That's not my dad. My dad is downstairs."

We didn't develop a bond until 2008, when I was able to use a cell phone. I used this phone every single day to impress upon my son's mind, there is no place I'd rather be than with him.

How do you forgive yourself for that?

–*Dontay Hayes K-88757*

Remorse Letter

This letter is a letter of remorse to my victims: Amy Fine, Shoko Fine, Brent Hirokawa, Dennis Ashley, Chadwick Ricks, Vanessa Tiana, Anne Grin Ruane, Sheila Peach, Scott Torrance, and Yvonne Alwag. Also the City of Torrance, Redondo Beach, Marina Del Rey, Ladera Heights, and Palos Verdes.

I can only imagine how terrified you all may be, pulling up to your own home after a long day of work, worried that someone may be in your home—or that some of your hard-earned possessions may be gone. I want to apologize from the bottom of my heart for invading your communities and homes. No one should ever have to live with the fear of their privacy being violated. I'm sorry for the sleepless nights you may still have even after all these years. For the negative stereotypes you may have of young black men who look and seem out of place in your neighborhood. For the constant paranoia you may have while you're at home with your family, and you receive a knock at your door from an unknown person. I can never give you back the peace and comfort you felt before I came and burglarized your homes, but I want to extend my deepest and most sincere apologies to you all.
I am truly sorry.

To Amy Fine and Shoko Fine, there's not a day that goes by I don't think about that day. The trauma and fear you must live in every day. To come home from work and see two young men taking possessions out of your bedroom while your daughter lays asleep downstairs—I must assume this was disgusting and terrifying. To you two in particular, I want you to know how sorry I am. I'm sorry for pushing you the way I did, Amy Fine, and fleeing with your belongings I'm sure you worked hard for. I am even more apologetic to you, Shoko Fine. I didn't even know you were home. I can imagine how scared you may be to be home alone now. I'm sorry to you both for the sleepless nights, the trauma, and the terror. I hope one day, if you haven't already, you'll find peace—my sincerest apologies.

–*Charles Johnson G-44141*

The Home They Built Around Me

A barren cell
A hole in hell
And I sit here all alone.

For one small crime
I pay with time
Where lights glare night and day.

And though I rage
And pace my cage
I still must stay and pay.

My body cramps
With cold that's damp
And it chills me to the bone.

I can hear the fling
Of the metal ring
Of keys and metal locks.

The scrape of feet
Upon concrete
As guards patrol the blocks.

Convict knives
That take human lives.
No jungle holds more danger.

And every day
That comes my way
Each man remains a stranger!

I watch my back
Cause there's a lack
Of men who can be trusted.

You know I'll kill
And I do I will
Before it's me that's dusted.

They came today
To take away
The man who lived next door.

To end his strife
He took his own life
He couldn't take it no more!

Now it's quiet here
Upon my tier
Since death has claimed another.

We're all wondering
Who'll be next
I hope it's not me, brother.

I don't know who
To tell this to
Cause most are only verses

That don't say much
Of anything
And most are only curses.

So if something fatal
Should ever come my way
Someone take my life.

Just tell my mom
I loved her so
And also tell my wife

That I was glad
For what we had
And all they've done for me.

And though I'm gone
One thing lives on
"My love eternally."

My one desire
Should I expire
Is that no one cry for me.

Just hold my mom
Within your arms
And tell her I'm finally free.

Until then I still remain... Pony Boy

—*Abel Maldenado E-97600*
(Maldenado was stabbed two weeks after writing this poem)

Enrique and Marisa Sanchez

How can I properly ever express to you—Enrique, Marisa, and the family—my remorse for the reckless and dangerous actions I committed prior and on November of 2005. You both are my family and I failed to recognize what I had. I was a lost boy and very selfish towards everyone. I not only offended you in an unacceptable manner, but the trauma I put you through makes me feel awful. Enrique, you have every right to be upset toward my actions and me. I took toward you: the emotional pain, fear, shock, and suffering I caused along with the trauma you have lived with all these years. The sudden and disturbing effect you felt the very moment I victimized you. I am remorseful for putting you through such an experience no one ever should. I know now that from that day on your life changed forever, and the thought of me shooting at you makes me feel sick. I can feel your vulnerability today. I'm truly sorry, Enrique, for all that I have caused you.

"How my daughter will grow up without her uncle in her life." (Marisa)

For the past 13 years I have lived with this thought, always mindful of its presence, and always motivated by the humiliating discomfiture of my role in your lives. Marisa, I could hear the sorrow in your voice when you spoke about my unborn niece, Dayanara, growing up without her uncle in her life. I could feel guilt churning in my guts as your words painfully found me. I put you both in a very traumatic experience. You raised me the best you could and always have been there for me. I acknowledge that now. I am ashamed of the stress I caused you. The fact I'm no longer in your life must be a daily struggle. I'm sorry for what I've done and how I put you between your husband Enrique and myself. I love you. Now every opportunity to do better, even the smallest encounters with others, are chances to show kindness, gratitude, and assistance, qualities I received from you as a child that have awoken in my heart after a decade. I had it deeply concealed. It's a reminder of you and it makes me a better human being today.

–*Edwin Medrano F-51692*

Untitled

My name is Jimmy McMillan. I am currently serving my 21st year of a 28-to-life sentence for the murder of Melvin Raynor. I was a few months removed from my 20th birthday when the tragedy occurred. I was spiraling down a dark and unforgiving road. I am in no way trying to make excuses. But I had no direction, no ambition in my life at that time. I was just released from prison, sentenced to 16 months for possession of marijuana that wasn't even mine! Again, I'm not trying to give excuses, but I felt the system hadn't given me a fair shake and swallowed me up and spit me out. So when I got released, I had changed, and not for the better. I was angry, disenchanted, felt powerless. I tried to get a job but was rejected due to my prison priors.

Allow me to express a brief history of my upbringing.

I was born in Seaside, California to a single-parent home. My mother was 18 when she had me. I have two sisters: one older by two years, one younger by two years. We all have different fathers. By the time my mother was 20 years old, she had three kids and no intention, nor motivation, to be a parent. My two grandmothers mostly raised me. My first four years, my grandmother on my father's side took me in and raised me as her own. My mother would drop me off to her and be gone for extended periods of time. This was fine with G-moms because she was well established in her community and church; she had her own house and big family. I was loved and treated as a vital part of that family dynamic, being the first grandchild. However, shortly after my fourth birthday, my mother took me from my G-moms home and we left the state. I didn't see my G-moms for another 35 years.

We moved around a lot, never staying in one place more than a year or two. More often than not, my two sisters and I would end up with my mother's mother. My grandmother on my mother's side of the family was a stark contrast to my father's mother. She was strict and uncompromising and quick to anger, which often led to physical abuse in the form of discipline called "whippings." Everyone call her "mom."

When I was six years old my uncle came to live with us—us being my grandmother and all her grandkids, and most of her kids as well. My mother was not living with us at the time. My uncle had just been released from prison. One night my uncle came into my room and sexually assaulted me. I tried hard to fight him off, but I failed. I just remember being helpless and the pain. I couldn't understand why he would do this to me. I was a six-year-old boy and he was a twenty-something man. It's so vivid and painful to think about, let alone write about. I kept it suppressed for all these years. I remember telling my grandmother—she responded by slapping my face and telling me to stop lying. I knew I would get no help.

A few nights later my uncle came into my room. I had been sleeping with a long butcher knife. He saw my weapon and, no doubt, could've taken it from me. He probably was about to do just that. Perhaps he saw the fear and anger in my eyes. I remember I was scared. I remember him looking at me and laughing, then turning and leaving me alone. I had lost all reasons to smile. My innocence was ripped away from me. That day I knew hate.

From elementary all through high school, we never went to the same school more than two years. I just stopped trying to make friends, because when I did we would just move and they would become memories. I wanted to fit in, to belong... somewhere.

My childhood was marred in violence and abuse. I remember the fear fondly. My mother and grandmother would beat my sisters and I for any infraction or slight, deserved or not. And I'm not talking about being hit with hands or belt. I'm talking bare-assed extension cords or switches from trees. We used to get these "whoopings" or "whippings" almost daily. I never understood this "ritual," especially when there were no explanations accompanied for the admonishments. Just the deed and then, after, a punishment enforced.

We didn't go out for weeks, sometimes months. No TV, no friends over, and chores, always more chores. I spent most of my childhood on punishment—and all of my adult life in prison. I've been "locked up" all my life one way or another.

Despite all this, I was never in trouble with the law. No juvenile detention centers, no youth authority. I was a decent student. At the age of 15, I fell in love with the game of basketball. By the time I was 17, I was one of the best in the whole state! I realize now that basketball was like a family. I constantly searched to fit in anywhere. When I found that bond, that love, I cherished it. In reality, basketball took me away from all the bad things I was going through at home. On the hoop court, I was free.

I was well on my way to getting a full-ride scholarship to play ball. College scouts took notice during my summer league play; they wanted to see me play for my senior year. I lived with my mother at the time. I did well in school for my last year.

Then, right before our basketball season started, my mother and I got into a heated argument about my little sister. She was 16 at the time. My mom used to go to nightclubs on the weekend. I would keep an "eye" on my sister. She wanted to go to a friend's house (a boy). I told her "No." She tried to sneak out. I stopped her. But eventually she snuck out anyway. I just locked the doors when she tried to come back in. She called our mother and told her I put her out in the rain! (It was raining also.)

My mother came home angry and misinformed. She started yelling and swinging on me. I was 17 and angry myself. We had a heated argument and she kicked me out. I believed she only kicked me out because she could no longer whip me with switches and cords. I left. I had no idea this moment in time would alter my path and send me down an uncharted abyss. This would ultimately lead to a man's death and me sentenced to life in prison.

I went back to Oakland to stay with my grandmother. I tried to enroll into a new school, my 5th in high school alone. However, the school would not allow me to enroll because my mother had informed the school in San Diego I had "run away." She failed to say she had kicked me out. The school's policy was to not release transcripts for runaways; my mother would not sign the papers saying I wasn't one. My grandmother tried to convince her, but she flat-out refused. I was devastated.

Not only would I not graduate but more important to me was that I couldn't play basketball! That meant there was no chance to impress the college scouts. For two months my grandmother and I tried. By then I had turned 18 and thought my dreams were shattered. I stewed in my own depression, stuck in my grandmother's apartment with nothing to do. My passion derailed.

Right outside my grandmother's apartment building, some guys I knew were selling marijuana. I began hanging out at first, but then found myself right along with them. By the summer of 1994, instead of graduating high school and going to college, as I had planned, I entrenched myself in the marijuana trade. The block, or "turf," as we called it, became my family. Soon I began looking at these guys as more family than my own.

The first time I got arrested for selling weed I had been given probation and a drug diversion class. I was to report back to the judge to show I had indeed signed up for the class. When I got arrested, I had seen how I hated being locked up. Again I felt helpless, not in control of my life. I made the conscious decision to leave the drug trade. It wasn't worth the trade-off.

The day I got out, I immediately went to comply with the judge's decree. As I was walking home from the bus stop, a police officer who patrolled our block pulled me over. Every instinct in me told me to run. But I had made up my mind I was done with that life. Still when I was dealing I used to run on him. He would give chase but never catch me. I vividly remember him rolling up on me just a week earlier. He was in the car ready to jump out. I kept walking, ready to break as soon as the door opened. He told me, "I'm going to get your ass before Christmas."

Now, as I was coming back from a court appointment, the police officer jumped out and grabbed me, then slammed me on his car. I did not resist, I clearly stated I hadn't done anything wrong. He handcuffed me and put me into his back seat. I told him that I was going home and I wasn't in the "game" any longer. I tried to show him my paper signed for the judge, which I was going to court to present to that judge in a few hours.

He took my paper, balled it into a wad, and tossed it to the ground. He drove me back to the "block." I had been on the next street, trying to avoid walking down the street where we sold. He parked on the spot and went into the very backyards that we did our business. He came out the yard with a brown bag and poured the contents on the trunk of his car. I could clearly see little sacks of weed. I also clearly saw these sacks of weed were not from our spot. I had never seen them before. I knew we didn't serve the small bags. We only served in bigger denominations of 20s and 50s.

What I couldn't clearly see was this officer of the law was going to plant this weed on me. He stated in his report he had observed me throughout that day "selling" to various peoples. Even though I had proof, and several witnesses from the college where I had been to sign up for the drug-diversion class, it was my word against his. Since I was on probation, no one would hear me—not the judge, not my own public defender. I was shipped to the pen for some weed that wasn't even mine, on the same day I was trying to change my life.

I was 19 and again felt powerless and betrayed. When I got out of prison after 16 months, I couldn't get a job and had no prospects. My attitude was, "I'm damned if I do and damned if I don't." I then started selling even harder drugs without remorse. I had been robbed once, so now I carried a gun.

One night on March 1, 1996, a guy I knew from the weed spot was walking past my spot. He asked me to come with him because some people owed him money. He sold crack, so I assumed they were crackheads. I agreed. We walked down the block to an apartment I had known well. I used to cut and sometimes cook my dope there; I gave "testers" to the guy whose apartment it was. The guy knocked on the door. Someone looked out the window. Clearly, he saw two hooded, black-clad figures and wouldn't open the door. He even asked, "Who is it?" staring right at us.

The guy I was with said "It's us." I was immediately confused— every fiber in my being said to leave. This wasn't right. The door opened and the guy burst in. I followed with gun in hand. He went straight into the back room, despite there being four people in the front room. I told the people they owed my boy his money. I ordered them to get on the floor.

One guy I later found out was named "Heavy D," better known as Melvin Raynor. He was a huge man, well over six feet and 300 pounds. He clearly didn't want to comply. He flat-out refused my order. I hit him with my gun on top of his head and pushed him down to the ground. He still didn't go to the ground, he snarled and stared me down. The others in the room, all of which I'd known except for him, were pleading with him to do as I said. He finally did. I was angry about his confrontational attitude. But he made me realize something: What the hell was I doing here? Clearly, these people were all crackheads; the whole apartment reeked of the fresh crack smoke. It was the first of the month—any money they had had gone to the dope man. I had even sold them some crack earlier that very day! I had a moment of clarity. Something wasn't right.

Then the guy whose apartment it was, Cedric Johnson, said to me, "Hey, just do what y'all came to do and leave." I knew then that this was something else.

I went into the back room. The guy I came with had a person under a dirty blanket. I said to him, "What's going on, man?"

"Hey, just go watch them," he said.

"Nah, I'm out," I told him. "You either with me or not. I'm gone."

I turned to leave. As I went into the front room again I immediately noticed the guy Heavy D wasn't on the ground. In fact, he was standing near the door. Clearly, he and the rest could've left. But he was just standing there. I stated loudly, so my acquaintance could hear me: "I'm leaving." I told Heavy D, "Get the fuck away from the door." He moved aside a few steps. I just wanted to leave. I opened the door to do just that when it happened. Heavy D rushed me. I had the door open, pulling it toward my body, with my back to him. He slammed into me, causing the door to slam shut. He punched me in the face and grabbed my arm that held the gun. I was stunned, not really by the blow but the fact he would do that, knowing I was leaving. I could clearly hear the other people yelling at him to "just let him leave."

I was flabbergasted—thinking this dude's crazy for trying to take the gun from me. Even though he outweighed me by more than 100 pounds, I knew I couldn't let him get the gun. We struggled, the gun literally going back and forth between our bodies. Like every scene in any movie, TV show, or play, the gun went off. Neither one of us moved, fearing somebody was hit.

After a second, which seemed like an eternity, Heavy D began to slump and grabbed his chest. As he slid down my body, still clutching my arm, the gun went off again. I saw the bullet go harmlessly into the ground. Relieved it wasn't me that was shot, I was also horrified I had shot someone. I hadn't even fired a gun before, not in fun or by aiming at empty cans. Then I got angry he would attack me as I was leaving. I spat at him and ran out into the night, leaving him still clutching his chest. I had no idea he would bleed to death. The people in the house all ran out—not one called an ambulance or the police. They were too busy trying to remove all contraband from the apartment.

I drove back to the scene three hours later. A crowd had gathered, ambulance and police cars mulled around. As soon as I pulled up, medics wheeled out Melvin's body under a sheet. I truly believed the guy I was with had come out and shot him; I didn't think the bullet in his right upper chest/shoulder could've killed him. I later found out in pre-trial that the bullet hit his clavicle bone, veered off, and nicked his heart. He bled out.

I also found out the guy I had come with had set this whole thing up. He had come to rob the person he had in the backroom of her income tax money. And the guy Cedric Johnson was in on it! In fact, the only persons who probably didn't know what was going down were the woman they'd set up, Melvin, and me. We were unwitting pawns in a game that went horribly wrong.

I confessed to the murder of Melvin Raynor. I told the detectives everything that happened, except I didn't identify the guy I was with. I kept his name out of it. Despite the incident being manslaughter, the District Attorney charged me with murder and one felony robbery. This despite the fact I didn't know anything about the robbery, nor was I there for that. At first the people who were there that night told the police in a statement what essentially happened. But by the time of my pre-trial, all of this changed. Suddenly I was the ringleader trying to rob them all. They claimed Melvin tried to "escape" when I shot him in the back. Here I was being lied about once again.

I eventually took a deal for 28-to-life to avoid the death penalty, which was more likely because of my confession.

Twenty-one years later I am trying to change my path, make better decisions. I used to make excuses this wasn't my fault. But that's what they were—excuses. I made all the decisions to put myself in these positions, for the consequences to trap me in my helplessness. I now make better decisions. I'm always aware of my poisons and my medicines. My quest for redemption has begun, and it will last the rest of my days. I not only do this for my family, who I've lost while in prison: R.I.P. "Mom" (grandmother) and Vivian (mother). But also for Melvin Raynor and his family, the victims.

Hopefully, one day I can prove to all who know me that I am more than a statistic of circumstance.

–Jimmy McMillan P-31432

Nigga Blues

I was bullied...
Before the cyber-minds and escape keys
I had to throw blows or bloodied nose
From older kids who didn't like my skin tone
Ravished from both sides
Wasn't quite white, but light enough to bruise...
Ego's ˜ From African Booty Scratchers
And Jigga boo's ˜ The Nigga Blues
This is the interlude ˜
Sweeter the Juice
I got mocked for my Lighter Hues
Boxed in, but where do I fit?
If Black is beautiful, why do I feel so ugly?
Ostracized for my awkward eyes
Chocolate ties I tried to cut when mixed Breed
And mutt was spewed from Black ducks
That bruise like tattoos ˜
Ooze ˜ Eggplants and Coons
This is the Nigga Blues.
Whose dark days for decades
Can compare?
Centuries of despair in this air...
Toxic like trips from Slave ships
Tainted ˜ one drip of Black Blood
I'm Black balled
Well you can kiss my Black Balls.
Choose...
No disrespect to the Natives or Jews
But this the Nigga Blues.

—Jimmy McMillan P-31432

Putrid Petals on the Whims
of a Withered Stem...

Sunlight shines in the guise of imperfections
There is dignity in darkness,
Even for a dying rose

Blunted thorns, roots no longer rooted
Secluded splinters on the moons of many winters
Noble poise in the face of a bitter cold
Even for a dying rose.

Seedlings glimmer with the hopes of a new day,
Vibrant with the whispers of tomorrow...
Todays are no longer promised
The skies weep with the essence of lost souls,
Let the light be your guide
In the guise of a dying rose.

–Jimmy McMillan P-31432

Poem Cry

I can't see em coming down my eyes
So I had to make this poem cry
This pen bleed
This paper scream with emotions with hopes it makes
Us free...
Can you relate to feeling faceless in a sea of faces
No more than a nomad on a path that went nowhere fast
Cuz we're still judged by the deeds of our past...
What does the future hold?
When our presence is evident in every element
And they tell us as long as we in prison, we irrelevant
Cuz it's hard to bloom on these crowded rooms where it's
Often dark—
And searching for light can take a lifetime—
If ya lost ya spark—
Lost in thought—so I often thought I couldn't smile
For my inner child—What-up lil homie?—it's been awhile
You are seen. Like the vestige of a dream
Where every deed is magnified like the ripples in a stream
And it seems we've seen so many nightmare scenes
That it doesn't take a horror to make us scream
Holla!
Pain is love—and it's a thin line between that and hate
And it's not too late to be strong enough to subtract the hate
Long as you add the love—give everything you have to
Love—and ya house of healing becomes a house of love
And that's what's up! I couldn't see em coming down my eye
So I had to make this poem cry.

—Jimmy McMillan P-31432

Realization

A bright light flashes,
The window crashes,
I'm wide awake and shivering cold, feeling groggy—
Then BAM! I get hit but feel no pain,
Dazed and confused says my brain,
It's a flashback but I'm not in my body—
I'm staring at myself through someone else's eyes,
Hot Cheetos on the floor, anger on his face, tears falling,
   I guess I cry,
A few seconds pass, I realize I'm my wife, and the room get foggy—
Now I'm outside, it's wet and chilly,
Walking down the street contemplating if he's going to kill me,
It all starts to slip away into a helicopter view, vision godly—

A bright light flashes,
The window crashes,
I'm at home cleaning up some chips, feeling filthy—
Then BAM! The realization hits me,
I just experienced what my wife went through with me,
Drop to my knees, eyes flooding, I'm feeling guilty—
How can I do this to the woman of my dreams,
Over something so petty as who's her favorite team,
All because we were drinking, my thoughts are all negative, oddly—
We're both Reds fans but this night she was claiming Dodgers,
Wish I could take it all back and apologize but why bother,
The dream evaporates, I wake up to realize... about me there's
   nothing godly.

—Daniel Newman A-16548

Trailer Park

Trailer park, trailer park, the place I call home/
The only place I've grown to know/
Thoughts of shame and embarrassment flood my mind/
My dirty little secret I was bound to hide/
No way I'd let the other kids see the status of my living/
So I dressed nice, acted friendly and giving/
Till one day a beautiful girl asked "me!" out/
Even invited herself to "Sit on my couch"/
That was the day I'd come to regret/
Because she seen where I lived and quickly left/
I was shocked and stunned, left like a fool/
Dreading tomorrow, the last day of school/
I vowed that night to not be the same/
From this point on I will not be ashamed/
The creator of the new me, is that girl to blame/
I've stepped it all up and introduced mac'ing to my game/

–Daniel Newman A-16548

When the street lamps come on

When the street lamps come on, it's time to go in.
Our parents didn't want us in the dangers of the night.
During the nighttime is when it all begins.
Illegal activity, "Ding!" goes the light.
I call two persons, it's just me and my friends.
Strolling through the hood, also known as the Trailer Park.
Tagging on the walls: Cans, Markers, and Pens.
Feeling like we're badasses unseen through the dark.
Dressed in all black, in the darkness we blend.
I and Spooky have knives, Demon has the strap.
Each one of us fearless, so we pretend.
A random man approaches so Demon busted a cap.
A loud crack, the guy falls and we turn the bend.
Everything goes fast, my mind can't think.
Suddenly the hood becomes unknown, like a fen.
Looking down the street, it all starts to shrink.
Sirens in the distance, thinking this is the end.
I tell the homies "let's get back to the pad."
We stash the strap and get home right at ten.
As we get to the door, it opens and there stands my dad.
Disappointment on his face, he said the word "Again?"
Unable to speak, no words come to mind.
Glancing up and down, asking himself "Why him?"
A Fucked up feeling is the only thing I could find.
When the street lamps come on, it's time to stay in.

–Daniel Newman A-16548

All Sales Are Final

The attitude
about my situation,
it strikes some as weird.
After all, I'm serving life
and have done so now
going on fifteen years.
"Don't you ever want to get
out?" they ask. "What about
all you are missing; all life's
niceties—surely there is
something in the free world
you miss—a decent meal; a
relationship; the choices not
found in prison?" And I can
only smile my self-conscious grin,
and wonder if my eyes look opaque.
Sometimes I try to explain my
thinking: that this is my life,
the one I bought, and am paying for.
But it doesn't register, so instead
I say, all sales are final, and
leave it at that.

—Patrick Nolan

Little Monkey Man

He grips between trembling hands wet with bath water,
a stiff bristle brush. He is six years old, and tears
run in rivulets down plum-colored cheeks. With cleanser,
he begins to scrub the soft black skin of his legs;
it hurts, but after awhile, the whitewashing numbs. He wants
to be clean, to never again worry about getting locked in
a cage. Sweat mixes the cleanser with blood; his tiny
frame spasms with frustration; his skin gets darker...

He's a "Little Monkey-Man" and "belongs in a cage,"
or at least, that's what the white kids say.

–Patrick Nolan

Dearest Mom,

Today is your birthday and I can't even call to wish you a happy b-day or send you a birthday card. It's been a long time since we celebrated your birthday together. I'm sorry I can't be out there with you on this day. Instead I'm going to write you this letter to let you know how I feel.

Mom, last night I saw you. You were young and beautiful and we lived in a big beautiful house. You held my tiny hands in yours and showed me around to your friends, letting them know how smart and handsome I was—and that one day I would grow up to be an educated and successful person. Looking up I could see your face filled with joy as you spoke so proudly of me. This made my tiny mind so happy because you were happy. I never imagined I would ever let you down.

I woke up in the morning and realized it was all a dream; staring down at me was a picture of you stuck to the bottom of the bunk above me. I looked at your face in that picture and realized you were not young anymore. There were gray hairs on top of your once beautiful black hairs. There are so many wrinkles around your worry-free eyes. Your beautiful smile still showed, but I wondered if your smile was just to hide the pain you feel inside.

The more I look at your picture now, the more I realize how much I have hurt you. I'm sorry I let you down and I'm sorry I can't be there for you or my siblings. It's not your fault I'm here—you're not to blame on how I choose to live my life. Sometimes I stay up all night crying inside, wishing I could put my foolish pride aside and let out all the pain I feel for letting you down.

I know you can't hear me crying, but it's there. I cried many times for you... I'm sorry I let you down.

Your Son,
M. D.

A Life in Prose

Awakening

I got off the bus to stand in front of this large looming ugly building with tall fences. I stood in line for what seemed like hours, only to be met by an overweight man, kneeling down and looking at me with a smirk and rotten, yellowed stained teeth.

"Now be a good boy and open your jacket," the man said. I could feel, even at three years old, a menacing ugliness in his voice.

Once I entered the prison and saw my mother, all my feelings of abandonment and anger left me. Grandma, my four-year-old sister, and five-year-old brother were with me. The sadness left our cherub faces, replaced with smiles and the immediate babble of the last month of school, neighborhood goings-on, and how Kathy, the neighborhood flirt, was nice to us. She was especially nice to me, since I thought she was pretty and I had a crush on her.

It would be years later when Kathy's beauty would fade and drugs would grip her so bad she'd be reduced to prostitution.

Grandma

Grandma had been given the task of taking care of my siblings and I while my mother was in federal prison. Grandma did a wonderful job. She was kind, patient, and loving. However, it was hard on her to take care of us, especially since we were poor.

In those days the only income that came into the house were the jobs that Grandma would do, like cleaning other people's houses.

The Greens were very understanding and kind. They gave Grandma odd jobs around their house so she could earn a few extra dollars to make ends meet. They lived a few houses away from our duplexes. The Greens were very nice to us, too, although I suspected they felt sorry for us since we were the only kids in the neighborhood who had parents in prison.

Happy Living

We lived in an old six-unit duplex on a slope, three units on one side and three units on the other side. We had one small bedroom and one small front room, which my siblings and I used as a bedroom to sleep. All three of us would share the same bed. My grandma shared her room with my teenage uncle, Smooth Tony. I was told he earned this name because he was smooth with the ladies—although I never saw him but with one girl, and she was no Kathy.

There was a small kitchen about the size of a hallway, five-by-ten feet. There was also a bathroom with a toilet, sink, and shower crammed into a space of about five-by-seven feet. My neighborhood was on a long dead-end with all kinds of characters. There were gangsters, thieves, robbers... all shades of people. We were of the low-income variety, which society wanted nothing to know about or do with. Yet this was my home and neighborhood. I loved every part of, warts and all. I knew nothing else.

Candy Land

Candies were my weakness. Every once in a while my brother and I would take a long walk to the big store. The store had candy in the front entrance for all to see. Easy pickings for a hungry kid like me. Food was limited and candy was a luxury I couldn't afford. I would take a candy bar once a week. In my mind I justified my actions. The store was a big store and it could take a small loss. Boy was I wrong.

Everyone knew everyone in the area. The store clerk knew Grandma. She had a tab with the store and once a month, she'd pay the bill. As fate would have it, I was with her as she paid the bill. The store clerk looked at me with disdainful eyes as Grandma walked away to talk to someone. The clerk leaned forward to get close earshot and said, "You little punk, your grandma knows you steal candy. She pays for it when she pays her monthly bill."

I was mortified and ashamed—the woman I adored and respected so much had been let down and disappointed by me. She worked hard to put a roof over our heads, food in our bellies. Here I was, stealing from her. Grandma's beautiful character never allowed her to say a word about it. But I could see the disappointment in her eyes. I never stole again!

I was six when my mother got released from prison. It was a happy day. The sun shone brighter, the wind blew a soft cool breeze as the leaves swayed back and forth as if they were singing a happy song.

Mom lived with us all crammed into our tiny duplex. Yet all of us kids were never happier! Soon mom was working and looking for a place to move us away from the neighborhood I had grown to love so much.

Dark Days

We eventually moved away. Grandma and Smooth Tony stayed back in the duplex. Mom moved us in with some friends of hers who had kids our ages. But you could see in their eyes something was off. I just couldn't put my finger on it. We were new to this.

It's a funny thing about people. They can live in a supposedly better area, but that doesn't mean they will be better people. I learned this by the messed up people we lived with. Mom had really tried to give us a better. She'd go to work, and we would be left with her friends and their kids. Most of the time my siblings and I would be left in a room while the people who were supposed to be watching us indulged in activities that would have never been seen in my neighborhood.

One day, Mom came back early from work only to find the adults indulging in their activities. Needless to say, shit hit the fan. There was a lot of yelling, throwing things around and cursing. After the incident we quickly moved away.

Road Trip

The year had passed and soon I was twelve years old. It was the mid 1970s, summertime, with a severe heat wave. Many people around the country had died from it.

Mom had become religious in prison and stuck to it after she was released. We would attend church weekly. As a divorcee she had many suitors. It seemed all the single men were in church. My mom was very beautiful, but she wanted nothing to do with any of them.

There was one man who was kind to us, mainly because of his feelings for my mother. He was a good person—a portly single father who had children my age and younger. He often tried to take my mother out to dinner; she'd have none of it. Her focus was us kids and church.

That summer, he took his kids across the country in a motor-home. As it turned out, I was getting into trouble a lot. He offered to take me with his family on the trip across the country with them. He said it would be a good experience for me—he was right. To this day I have a vivid memory of that trip. Prior to this, I had never been outside of my area but for the brief moment we lived with that other family.

Beautiful Landscapes

Our trip would be a memorable one. The first stop was in Arizona at a trading post on the side of the highway. There was a young Native American, about 19 years old, working there. There was also an old white woman yelling at the young girl in a demeaning way, calling her a stupid Indian. Her words were so callous and vile it caught me off guard—especially coming out of what looked like a sweet grandma.

I had experienced racism in my life before, mainly in school and run-ins with the police. However, this was at an extreme level I had not seen or even known about. I would soon find out just how hateful and evil humans could be.

As our trip continued, I saw the different beautiful landscapes along the way. The scenery was awe-inspiring. I had never seen forests or landscapes like these. I was used to the concrete jungle with its large buildings, houses, apartments, and the occasional trees on the sidewalks. Nothing like this. It was as if I were in a different world. We mostly traveled at night because of the heat. I still got to see so much, and my world seemed bigger.

Eye Opener

Another stop, at a Texas rest stop, was an eye opener for me. It was midday and we had exited where there were souvenirs. I decided to buy my mother a souvenir spoon in every state we stopped at so I could share something of the trip with her. On this particular stop I went in the store, looked at the variety of spoons, and went to the counter to purchase the spoon I had chosen. There were two older people behind the counter who looked like sweet kind grandparents. They were smiling and laughing with the customers before me. I was feeling happy and joyous as it was my turn. I put my spoon on the counter. The older white-haired man said "Next," and looked past me as if he was looking for someone behind me.

"Right here," I said, with a happy grin. This time both white-haired grandparents looked past me as if I weren't there.
Just then I felt a hand on my shoulder. It was the family's friend. He said softly, "Let's go, we will buy it at another store." Just at that moment the older man put a sign in front of us that was on the counter, but I hadn't noticed it before. It read: NO DOGS, NO SPICS. I didn't know what spics meant! I later asked the family's friend what it meant. He told me it's a disrespectful term they call us. I pondered on that for some time. But that never stopped me from collecting spoons for Mom.

As we drove from state to state, I was able to see how beautiful this country is. At the same time, I met good people and I experienced real prejudice.

We continued to travel through southern states, across the Mississippi River to the border between North and South Carolina. That's where the biggest amusement park in the South is: Carowinds. It was a vast amusement park with every ride you could think of. It got late so we never got to finish enjoying the big place. We still had to drive to Virginia where my family friend's brother lived; he had a church where he was the pastor.

Ugliness

On the way to Staunton, Virginia, there was a protest ahead; the highway slowed to a crawl. As we got closer, we could see a TV crew out with their cameras. On one side there were black men, women, and children who were marching, but had stopped. On the other side there were people with white hoods and white robes, armed with guns and rifles. They were shouting profanity at the black people. All of a sudden, the white hooded people started shooting at the black people. Traffic stopped. The people started running away, many slipping in between the cars on the highway. Some had fallen from the gunshots. Sadly, some who had fallen were children.

All of a sudden, the side door of the camper we were in flung open. Two hooded men stood with their rifles at the ready.

"Where are they?" they shouted. "Did any of them come in here?"

They looked around, opened the bathroom door. This happened as we all stood frozen with the knowledge that at any sudden movement we could be victims. After searching, and realizing no one had run into the camper, they began to leave. One of them stopped and stared at us—curiosity and cold violence in his eyes. After a few long seconds, he turned away and left.

We finally made it to Staunton, Virginia in the Appalachian Mountains. Driving through the winding small roads, we passed a church with a sign that read: 10:00 AM WHITES ONLY SERVICE, 11;30 COLORED ONLY SERVICE.

Immediately I felt I was in a different world.

As we pulled over to stretch our legs and wash up, I went over to the restroom, not thinking about anything but using the restroom. As I was about to enter, a black man stopped me. I failed to notice the signs. Even the water fountains had signs. Though I was light-skinned, I was not white. I would have been arrested for using the white-only restroom or white-only water fountain.

The Civil Rights Bill had been passed several years before, but some places didn't care about this. Bad habits were hard to break. It was a time when racism was normal for some people. It was sad that anybody would still have that mindset—and I could be an afterthought.

Soon we met up with the portly man's brother. I even got to play baseball with the local white church kids. I noticed there weren't any black kids around. I asked about that—I was told they had their own baseball field.

The kids all looked like they were related, but they weren't. They were around my age. The only name that came to mind was "rednecks" because they had real red necks!

These kids weren't sure if I was Indian. Eventually they came to the conclusion I had no black in me. I had seen an ugly side of America. It was the first time I truly understood what it was like to be judged for the color of your skin. At that moment I wanted to leave. But I was from L.A. and my foolish pride got the better of me. I did feel my life was hanging in the balance. Nonetheless, I played ball with them, although I couldn't wait to leave.

The road trip experience was educational, despite the ugliness I witnessed and experienced. I learned a lot about myself. I saw things I never seen in my little neighborhood area. I had grown from a boy to a man that summer. I had seen the beauty of this country and the ugliness that it holds. This trip would shape me, unfortunately. I wouldn't grasp the significance until much later.

–Manuel R. Sanchez K-15621

Dear Younger Self,

I am writing this letter in the hope you will accept my advice and hard-earned knowledge.

I know your youngest memory of your mother was of visiting her at Terminal Island Prison. At four years old, you met a man who you didn't know was your father. Just as quickly as he came into your life, he left.

I know you never realized that growing up without your parents, or living in extreme poverty in a gang-infested neighborhood, were not normal. You never had new clothes. Your shoes had holes in their soles. But Grandma always did her best to keep you and your siblings clean and looking sharp.

When your mother was finally released from prison, she tried to move you to a better environment. But that environment was just as bad. By then, you had already made up your mind you can't count on anyone except yourself. You had taught yourself how to survive. So far you thought you made it.

Let me tell you now you will mess your life up, mostly because you thought you knew it all. You believed you knew more than your mother as well as every adult trying to give you positive advice. Your selfish ways led you to a life of heartache, and eventually the loss of your freedom. You think it's cool hanging out with your older homies, drinking and smoking weed. Those drugs will lead you to take harder and more addictive drugs. You think you will be able to say no to the hard drugs, but your ego will drive you to be seen as a down homie. This will lead you to forsake your common sense.

If you don't change your negative ways, one day you will be 53 years old and have already spent 36 years of your life in prison. At 27 years old, you will be sentenced to three life sentences, plus 50 years, all consecutive. At 27 you will be spending the next 23 years of your life in solitary confinement. There you will be pacing in your concrete box, like a wild animal, repetitive movements to nowhere.

You will be living trapped in your own mind, reliving your past over and over. You will not comprehend that the world has moved on without you. You won't receive a single visit in 19 years. Letters from your family and friends will trickle to a letter once a year. For some family members, the letters will stop altogether.

At 50 years of age, you will be allowed out of your tomb and placed back on the mainline. Your health will be failing. You will have to learn how to be around people, how to talk to people, learn how to hug your children again. You will have a host of hurdles to overcome just to function as a normal human being.

Your three daughters were only kids when you got busted. They grew up, got married, with kids of their own. You will miss out on all of this. You will miss the opportunity to wake them up, cook them breakfast, and take them to school. You will miss their graduations. You won't be there to give them away when they get married—or hold your grandkids in your arms.

When your youngest daughter visits you for the first time, she will come with her husband and your two grandchildren. She was so excited to see you she started to cry. At that moment, you thought you would hug her and wipe her tears. Instead all you did was look at her and pat her on the back. You see, life doesn't work right for you because you have been devoid of humanity for so long, you didn't know how to react.

Your life doesn't have to be like this. All you had to do was listen to the advice of people who cared about you. Stop thinking you know better, that you're smarter than others. Don't disregard their good advice as a sign of weakness. Stay away from those homies who want you to get in trouble with them. Especially stay away from those who do drugs. Even if you think you can help them, you won't be able to. Instead you will fall right into the same trap they're in.

I have one more thing to tell you—you will do all this time for crimes you didn't commit or even had knowledge of. This is what awaits you if you choose not to listen to those that want to help you. And stop blaming others for your bad choices or your upbringing.

Accept your part in the bad choices you have made so far and what has happened in your life. But if you choose to still be hard headed, then there is a cell waiting for you.

Sincerely,

You

Finding Me

I may not be as articulate as others, but allow me a moment to do the best I can to express my sincere feelings of remorse for my immature and reckless actions.

I fully understand a lot better now the lives I ruined, hurt I caused, and the ripple effect of my actions, As a man now looking back, I am gripped by pain and remorse because of the devastation I caused so many people. I am truly sorry for what I did. I know words are not enough. All I can say is I am trying to do better. I let people influence and pressure me whom I looked up to, whom I should not have. I focused only on my survival. Certain things, whether I agreed or not, I had to do because I was told to do it. I saw no other option. Now I do.

I hope I am not sounding like I'm making excuses for my actions. My purpose is not to excuse it. I'm only trying to give insight into my mind state and why I made such bad choices. Even though I was led by bad influences, and saw no other options at that time, I did have a choice to say no, and accept the consequences of my fate. But I was only a kid—scared to be the man I am now.

I've matured. I accept full responsibility for my mistakes. I have devoted myself to change.

Not only am I remorseful about what I did to Mr. Mercado and Ms. Wilson, who were people with family and friends of their own, I also have a conscience—I live with that pain and regret every day. I regret the devastation I placed on my son having to grow up without a father present. And having to deal with the fact that at age 17 his father killed two people and caused so much misery and trauma. I know I disappointed him. My family as well as my parents, who have both passed since I've been in prison, all expected more from me. It took me time to grow up. Unfortunately it was after their passing.

In the last several years I have attempted to right some of those horrible wrongs. Over this 25-year incarceration, I've matured my outlook on life intellectually and morally. I've gained a stronger sense of moral ethics and scholastic credentials. I want you to know I am no longer that damaged, scared yet aggressive 17-year-old kid I was back in 1993 when I first committed those acts.

—*Frank Showel*

Tears of a Kid

I am currently in a correctional facility for the crime of kidnapping, torture, and robbery. Please allow me this opportunity to share my story of how I got to this point of my life, serving 24 years in prison.

I grew up in a loving family, destined to succeed in life. I grew up in a big family—I had parents, three sisters, and two brothers. Unfortunately one of my brothers passed away when I was still a baby. I can't imagine the pain my parents went through when they lost their beautiful Angel.

Growing up I hated myself. I never felt like I belonged. I struggled in school and I was always getting in trouble. I could never understand why I couldn't do the schoolwork. I got held back from the second grade and watched all my classmates move on. That had a big impact on my life. I started telling myself I was a stupid kid. With no way to communicate with my parents, I held everything in. I acted out at a young age. I was a troubled, insecure, shy, and lonely kid with learning disabilities.

My troubles really started in the fifth grade when I started smoking marijuana and hanging out with the troubled kids who I identified and related with. I began fighting a lot and getting suspended from school. Acting out in school and fighting made me feel accepted—until it came time for my mom to pick me up. I would go back to being shy, insecure, and lonely. I prepared myself to get disciplined by my mom or brother. I wouldn't understand why this was happening to me.

My bad behavior worsened when I began hanging out with my cousins, who were involved in gang activity. They took me in and embraced me. I would smoke weed and do other hard drugs with them. They were my role models. I looked up to them and wanted to be just like them. My trouble continued at home and school. My parents had lost all control of me. I was fully involved in using meth, smoking marijuana, and gang activity. I had distanced myself from my family. All I cared about were my "homies." They gave me guidance, respect, and love, things I didn't feel I had growing up.

Not having that guidance or approval also had an impact on me. It led me to find guidance and approval from negative influences. This led me to joining a gang, to indulging in and selling drugs, hurting my family and innocent people, stealing cars, and staying out all night in my neighborhood. Seeing my mother cry at night destroyed me. I hated myself for that—but I didn't have the tools to change. All my hardships and insecurities—the comfort I felt among gang members and my excessive need to be accepted, loved, and respected by them—led me to commit the crime of kidnapping, robbery, and torture. I pleaded guilty to the charges and accepted a 24-year prison term.

As I sit here in prison a changed man, strong in my faith in Jesus Christ, certified as a customer service specialist and all facets of telecommunications, I reflect on the little things I miss about growing up: My mother's delicious cooking, her hugs and kisses, her caring for me every time I got sick. Also kissing my mother good night, my dad taking me to my baseball and basketball games, walking on the green grass barefoot, getting together with my family on the holidays. All the things I took for granted.

To the reader I say this: When you think you are down for good, simply start affirming what an advantage it is to have hit rock bottom. The bottom is as far down as I can go. The only direction from here is up. And up I am going.

—Anthony Valencia

Dear...,

I would like to take this time to express my deepest regrets for kidnapping, robbing, and torturing you. I know from that day on your life changed forever. I couldn't even imagine the hurt, pain, and fear you were going through—and the thought of never seeing your family again. The scars you carry on your body are a daily reminder of the torture you went through. You have to carry that forever—and I'm sorry.

I sit back and wonder of the pain I caused your family, not knowing if their dad, son, or brother was ever going to come back home. I'm sorry for the pain I inflicted. I was a young man that wanted to prove himself to his friends and cousins to be accepted. I'm sorry for all the shame I caused my community and my family. I've not been able to see my nieces and nephews grow up, not able to be there for my parents who are getting older and need help around the house.

As I sit here and wait for my freedom, I pray every night for you and your family to find peace. I pray that someday you could forgive me for what I did to you and your family.

Sincerely,
Anthony Valencia

Victim Letter

I wonder if you truly understand what you have done. In 1992, when you committed the selfish and senseless act that took my life, did you understand that blow to my head not only murdered me, but did my family unspeakable harm?

I never thought the last time I kissed my wife and children would literally be the last time. After spending time with my brother and friends, I had my heart set on having dinner with my wife that night. Because of you that will never happen again!

Do you understand you have taken a husband, provider, and friend from my wife? She will never hear my voice or even feel my touch as long as she lives. We will never laugh or cry together again. Do you understand the pain she will endure when she tells our children their father was murdered? Do you understand the loneliness she will feel because I'm not there?

In taking me, you took milestones: birthdays, holidays, and anniversaries. Or consider days like my children's graduations, marriages, births of grandchildren. All of these have been taken away. Even the simple joy of walking around the block will be empty because I'm not there.

Have you ever considered the hardship of my wife being a single parent? I was the sole provider. Who will pay the bills? She may eventually find love and remarry, but what of the troubled times until she does?

What about my children? They will miss me the most. Children need their father. It was my responsibility, my duty, to teach my son manhood and model it for him. I will never be able to cheer him on, pat him on the back when he succeeds. I will never be able to validate him as a man, let him know he's got it under control, to reassure him he measures up when he feels like he doesn't.

As for my little girl, who will be her protector? I won't be able to wipe away her tears, to tell her it's going to be okay when she experiences disappointment. What happens when she gets her heart broken? I won't be there to hold her in my arms and give her a father's comfort. I won't be able to promise her brighter days are ahead. I will never be able to show her a picture of a real man and how she should expect to be treated. This is important because a daughter usually marries a man like her father. I won't be there because of your selfish act. Do you understand that?

By not being there for every birthday, holiday, and special day, something will always be missing. I can't get over how much you've stolen from me. I will never see my children graduate school. I will never see my children get married and start families of their own.

Some things are just gone, never to return. Gone is the chance to walk my little girl down the aisle, to see my son marry his soul mate, and watch them have grandchildren. I will never get to hold them, spoil them, and create new traditions with them. We will never know each other except through pictures and shared stories. I can go on and on. I think you get the picture.

I wonder, do you understand what you have done to your family as well? The shame and depression, the wondering where they went wrong. The sleepless nights, all the missed meals, the worry and pain, all the shed tears. The longing to hold you, to protect you. Now they are helpless because they can't do anything about it. The only thing they can do is love, support, pray, and visit you. Birthdays, holidays, and special days are empty for them too, because you are not there. The truth is that you didn't just murder me and ruin my family, you ruined your life and family too.

For what?

A couple of bucks.

Here I lay...

Tough Guy

So you think you're tough,
and on your weakest day,
downright rough!

The take-no-shit kinda man,
in for murder, robbery,
and when you're feeling nice
a little mayhem!!

Yah, don't think I don't see you,
always looking hard,
constantly telling war stories
and how you can stroll any prison yard!!

Well you can leave that shit at the door,
my friend, all your loudmouth ways and such,
because to be honest with you partner,
that kind of crap never impressed me much!!

But if you really want respect,
and show what a big man you can be,
then join the "Inside Circle."
Here you can have a seat,
right next to me!!

Seems pretty easy don't it?
A candle, a carpet, a circle of men,
then step up on the plate and be honest—
we don't come here to pretend!!

Don't tell me you're scared,
your knees are knocking,
and your nerve is rattled!
You said you were a tough guy
ready for any battle!!

I'm not trying to pick on you,
because it's not easy for any of us here.
But I can say this to you my friend:
it takes a tough man to shed a tear!!

So let us sit and talk,
and maybe even find,
the soft side of your nature,
the real man,
the human "inside!!"

So come on tough guy,
put your fears aside,
jump in the middle of the circle,
take that magic carpet ride!!

Then when it's over,
the mask is down and there's nowhere to hide,
after all I've seen your wounds
and you've witnessed mine!!

That is the time,
right there and then,
when I'll be proud to call that
"Tough Guy" my friend!!

Statement by Cover Artist

My name is Alfredo Mayorga. I was born in Guadalajara, Mexico and resided in Venice, CA. I love to draw, play sports, and spend time with my family. My hope is for a world where no one goes hungry and everyone lives in peace.

I want to dedicate this artwork to all the men who are incarcerated but are trying to find a way to better themselves and society.